Celebrate!®

WEDDING CAKES

EDITED BY EUGENE T. AND MARILYNN C. SULLIVAN

WILTON ENTERPRISES, INC., WOODRIDGE, ILLINOIS

OTHER WILTON BOOKS

CO-EDITORS: Marilynn C. and Eugene T. Sullivan
PRODUCTION ASSISTANT: Ethel LaRoche
ART ASSISTANTS: Jim Artman, Ewald Weber
PHOTOGRAPHY: Tom Kasper
CAKES DECORATED BY:
    Norman Wilton
    Yvonne Disharoon
    Hoa Dong
    Marie Grainger
    Melanie Javate
    Marie Kason
    Susan Matusiak
    Betty Newman May
    Michael Nitzsche
    Eleanor Rielander
    Amy Rohr

TENTH PRINTING, JULY, 1991

Editorial mail should be addressed to:
    Wilton Book Division
    2240 West 75th Street
    Woodridge, Illinois 60517

Library of Congress Cataloging in Publication Data
Main entry under title:
Celebrate! Wedding Cakes
  1. Cake decorating, I. Sullivan, Marilynn
II. Sullivan, Eugene T. III Wilton Enterprises
IV. Wedding Cakes.
TX771.C38 1983   641.8/653   82-21814
ISBN 0-912696-23-0

Celebrate! Wedding Cakes
is published by Wilton Enterprises, Inc.

ASK ANY DECORATOR what she needs most to decorate beautiful cakes and the answer will be—*ideas*. And in your letters and comments you've told us you always need ideas for wedding cakes.

So here are one hundred exquisite cakes to fulfill your search for ideas. We've chosen the most beautiful cakes from *Celebrate!* annuals ... then added scores of exciting brand-new creations.

To make decorating easy, we've printed clear step-by-step directions for each cake that take you from the first flower to the final lovely vision on the reception table. Diagrams show you unusual constructions, close-up pictures explain details of trim.

We've even developed new products to make your cakes more dramatic as they save you decorating time. Lacy stairways, see-through pillars, frilly new ornaments and graceful wedding procession figures will add effortless beauty to even a simple cake.

I'm proud to present this new idea book to you. I know it will help to make decorating bridal cakes a joy!

Vincent A. Naccarato

VINCENT A. NACCARATO
President, Wilton Enterprises, Inc.

Celebrate! WEDDING CAKES

CHAPTER ONE

Grand Celebration Cakes

Here is a display of magnificent cakes designed to serve from 350 to almost 600 guests. Large as they are, intricate details and delicate color give them a graceful appeal.

There's a fascinating variety—imposing large single cakes, dramatic confections encircled by smaller satellite cakes, and most exciting of all, a group of stairway spectaculars. Multiple cakes are joined by lacy, lofty stairways for a single fabulous effect.

Surprisingly, every one is simple to decorate! Only basic techniques are needed, so even a novice decorator can achieve these super-size masterpieces. Imaginative construction gives each one a distinct personality.

DECORATOR'S BONUS! These Grand Celebration cakes offer a wealth of ideas for smaller cakes, too. The main cake or one of its satellites can be reproduced to be handsome on its own. Or servings of a large cake, like Cloud Nine (page 30), can be reduced by simply omitting the base tier.

AT LEFT: Stairway to the Stars, a decorator's triumph. Garlands and cascades of golden sweet peas adorn tiers linked by soaring stairways. For decorating directions, please turn the page.

Stairway to the Stars

A big beautiful extravaganza! Lacy stairways give drama, ruffly sweet peas add golden color.

Five cakes are joined by the stairways to give a single spectacular effect. Allow time to assemble the tableau on the reception table—but the decorating itself is easy.

ASSEMBLE YOUR ACCESSORIES

Arched pillar tier set
Kolor-flo fountain
Filigree fountain frame
Four 7" Corinthian pillars
Two 9" separator plates
Four Filigree stairways
Two Stairway bridges
Twelve Angel musicians
Bridal couple figures
Bridesmaid figures
Groomsmen figures
Frolicking cherub
Two Lazy daisy servers
Two 14" plates
  (from Tall tier stand)

Pipe royal icing sweet peas

Use pale and deeper yellow icing and tubes 104, 103 and 102 for varied sizes.

Prepare the tiers

MAIN CAKE. Base tier consists of two two-layer 16" round tiers. Stack them together with a 16" cake board between them for a finished height of about 6". Second tier is a two-layer 12" x 4" round. Top tier is a two-layer 8" x 3" round. Ice and assemble tiers with separator plates and 7" pillars.

On base tier, at center front and back, mark a 6½" half-circle about 2" down from top edge. Repeat half-circles on either side of first ones, making guides for large garlands. Join half-circles at sides of tier with smaller half-circles. These will serve as guides for garlands beneath stairways.

Divide 12" tier into sixths and mark near top edge. Divide 8" tier into tenths and mark 1" above base.

TWO-TIER SATELLITE CAKES. Base tiers are 12" x 4" two-layer rounds. Top tiers are two-layer 8" x 3" rounds. Replace plates on lazy daisy servers with 14" plates. Ice and assemble tiers on prepared servers.

Divide 12" tiers into sixths and mark near top edges. Divide 8" tiers into tenths and mark midway on sides of tiers.

SINGLE-TIER SATELLITE CAKES are two-layer 10" x 4" rounds. Fill and ice. Place on foil-covered cake boards. Divide in tenths and mark near top edges.

Decorate two-tier satellites

These two cakes are identical. Decorate base tiers exactly like 12" tier of main cake. On top tiers, pipe a tube 16 base shell border. Drop string guidelines from mark to mark, then pipe tube 16 zigzag garlands. Attach sweet peas at points. Pipe sweet pea borders at tops of tiers. First pipe a tube 104 sweet pea on top of cake, then a second on side of cake directly below it. Continue to complete ruffly border.

Decorate single-tier satellites

These are identical. Pipe tube 125 sweet pea base borders. The technique is the same as piping the side petals of the flower. Pipe a petal against side of cake, then a second one, just beyond it, on cake board. Continue around cake for this quick border.

Drop string guidelines for garlands from top edges of cakes. Pipe tube 16 zigzag garlands, then reverse shell top borders with same tube. Attach clusters of sweet peas within points of garlands.

Decorate the main cake

DO TWO LOWER TIERS as a unit. On 12″ tier, pipe a tube 18 top shell border. Edge separator plate with tube 16. Pipe a tube 18 rosette border at base. As bases for cascades, pipe zigzag diamonds with tube 16 at marks, extending over top of tier. Press in sweet peas, then attach more sweet peas at edges of diamond shapes.

ON 16″ TIER, pipe a tube 22 shell border at bottom, a tube 18 reverse shell border at top. Using half-circles as guides, pipe tube 18 zigzag garlands. Cover with sweet peas. Add tube 3 bows. Within each large garland use icing to attach two angel musicians.

ON TOP TIER, Use tube 16 to pipe a shell border at base, reverse shells at top. Drop string guidelines, then pipe tube 16 zigzag garlands. Add sweet peas at points.

Final trim and assembly

Assemble main cake with fountain and filigree frame on the reception table. You will need a table at least 3′ x 6′. Thin royal icing with corn syrup and pipe mounds at tops of 7″ pillars and press in sweet peas. Pipe zigzags of icing on triangular areas at top of arched pillars and press in sweet peas. Glue angel figures to lower separator plate and heap sweet peas at their feet. Place bridge within upper pillars and place bridal couple on it. Trim second bridge with flowers, attaching with dots of royal icing. Place on top of cake with cherub.

Arrange the five cakes on the table and have a helper hold the stairways above them while you adjust positions. Set stairways in place, then trim with flowers, attaching with royal icing. Add figures of bridesmaids and groomsmen. Stand back to admire Stairway to the Stars! Omitting the top tier, it will serve 596 guests.

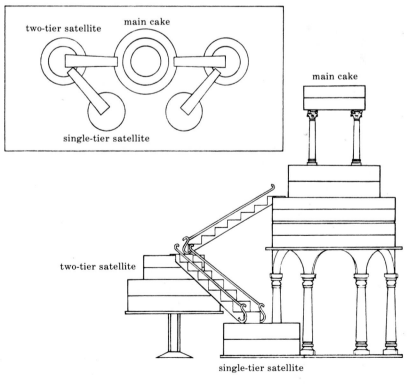

7

Tower of roses

A bride's dream of a cake that will dominate the reception and impress everyone who sees it. Five tiers rise in graceful dignity to almost four feet above the circling satellite cakes. Rhythmic curves of stringwork detail the tiers—sprays and garlands of pale apricot roses soften the elegant structure.

You'll find that the tall tier stand makes it easy to assemble this cake with no need for supporting dowels. The satellite tiers rest securely on the four-arm cake stand. After you've piped the roses, decorating is quick and easy, too—only basic techniques are combined to give Tower of Roses its beautiful effect.

ASSEMBLE YOUR ACCESSORIES. From the Tall tier stand you will need:

Four 12" plates and the four-arm stand (for satellite cakes)
16", 14", 12", 10" and 8" plates (for main cake)
Four 7¾" columns
One 6½" column
Four Frolicking cherub figures (for satellite cakes)
A Kissing lovebird sculpture (for top of cake)

Pipe flowers in advance

Use royal icing so the roses can be made well ahead of time to make decorating day easy. You will need a variety of sizes. For large roses, use tubes 127, 126 and 124. For top tier, and for tapering ends of sprays, pipe roses with tube 104.

Bake and assemble the tiers

The four satellite cakes at the base of the main cake are 10" round, each two layers for a height of 4". Bake five two-layer tiers for the main cake: 14", 12" 10", 8" and 6". Make all layers 2" high for a finished tier height of 4", with the exception of the top tier, 3" high.

Fill and ice with buttercream, using pale peach for satellite cakes, white for all other tiers.

PLACE SATELLITE CAKES on 12" plates. Assemble the four-arm cake stand with a 7¾" column. Attach 16" plate for base 14" tier. In ascending order, attach 14", 12" and 10" plates, using 7¾" columns. Below top 8" plate secure a 6½" column. Place iced tiers on plates. Take apart for decorating.

Decorate the cake

Use boiled icing for all trim. Simple star-tube borders and dropped stringwork are quick to do.

SATELLITE CAKES ARE IDENTICAL. Divide top edge of cake into 16ths, and mark. Drop a row of tube 3 strings from marks. Starting at center of curve, drop a second row of strings, then a third. On top of tier, pipe tube 13 scallops from mark to mark. Now pipe a tube 364 shell border at base, and a tube 362 shell border at top.

ON 14" TIER, divide and mark top edge into 24ths. Repeat markings on side of tier, 2" down from top edge. Drop tube 4 strings from mark to mark on side. About ½" below drop a second series of parallel string curves. Top points of curves with dots. On top of cake, pipe tube 13 scallops from mark to mark. Finish with a tube 32 shell border at base, tube 364 shell border at top.

ON 12" TIER, divide top edge into 18ths and mark. Drop a double row of tube 4 strings. Pipe a base border of curved "C" shells with tube 32. Pipe a tube 364 top shell border.

ON 10" TIER, divide and mark top edge into 18ths. Make a second series of marks on side of tier, about 2" down from top. Drop tube 4 strings from mark to mark on side, then add a second parallel series of strings just below. Top points of curves with dots. Pipe tube 13 scallops on top of tier from mark to mark. At base, pipe a tube 32 shell border, at top a tube 364 border.

ON 8" TIER, divide top edge into 14ths and mark. Drop tube 4 strings from mark to mark, then a second series of string curves, topping points with dots. Pipe a tube 32 curved "C" shell base border. Finish with a tube 363 top shell border.

DIVIDE TOP 6" TIER into 12ths and mark on side of tier 1" down from top edge. Drop double parallel strings with tube 3 and top with dots. Pipe a tube 19 base shell border, tube 363 border at top.

Put it all together

Now reassemble all decorated tiers on the tall tier stand.

ON TOP OF SATELLITE CAKES, form graceful horseshoes of roses, massing larger flowers at center, tapering to smaller roses at ends.

ON TOP OF 14" AND 10" TIERS, form four sprays of roses. Pipe a few tube 3 stems at ends of sprays, extending down sides of tiers. Finish sprays with smaller roses and buds.

ON 12" AND 8" TIERS, attach roses in a garland around edge of tier. Tilt each on a mound of icing to show them off at their best.

ON TOP TIER, form two little sprays of the smallest roses and buds, draping down on side of tier.

Use tube 68 and thinned icing to pipe leaves to trim all flowers on lower tiers. Change to tube 65 for leaves on top tier.

At the reception table, top each satellite cake with a little cherub figure. Crown the cake with the lovebird ornament. Tower of Roses stands ready for the guests' admiration and applause. It will serve 430, not counting the top tier.

Top of the World

A magnificent bridal cake, soaring to almost 40″ in height! Yet you will find it easy to decorate with simple techniques borrowed from the Philippine method. Pipe the flowers well in advance for a carefree day of decorating the cake.

ASSEMBLE YOUR ACCESSORIES. Since Top of the World consists of identical twin cakes, you will need two sets of many items.

Four 14″ separator plates
Four 8″ separator plates
16 Corinthian pillars, 5″ height
A complete stairway set
Kolor-flo fountain
Filigree fountain frame
One 12″ separator plate
   (for fountain)
Two 18″ separator plates
   (to support cakes)
Classique vase
Two Cherub fountains
Eight Angelinos
Two Heart base top plates
Bridal couple figures
Bridesmaid figures

PREPARE THE FOUNTAIN. Center the fountain on a 12″ separator plate and slip the frame over it. With a heated corsage pin, make four equally spaced holes in the base of the Classique vase. Pass light florists' wire through the holes in the vase and corresponding holes in the top tier of the fountain. Twist ends of wire to secure tightly.

Please turn the page

SPREAD WIRES,
PIPE PISTILS

TWIST WIRES

DRY FLOWERS UPSIDE DOWN

PIPE DAISIES

DAISY VARIETIES

Pipe the flowers

Use royal icing and the quick Philippine manner. Do pistils for daisies first. Cut about 18 stems, 6″ long, from fine florists' wire, twist ends into a cluster, then bend a tiny hook in other end of each wire. Insert a hooked end of wire into a decorating cone fitted with tube 7, squeeze lightly and pull cone away. Push wire cluster into a block of styrofoam to dry. Now, *holding wire upside down,* twirl it like a flower nail and pipe two or three rows of tube 1 stamens around tip of pistil.

Weight a cake rack on one end and hang *upside down* to dry—one hour or less, just to stiffen. After stamens are dry, pipe petals with tube 81, holding wire upside down again. Pull out a circle of petals, attaching each firmly to pistil, below stamens. Hang on rack *upside down* to dry. To vary the daisies, cover tip of pistil entirely with stamens or add two or three rows of petals for a fluffy effect.

THE CALACHUCHI is a tiny star-like flower. Pipe pistils with tube 5 in the same way as for daisy. Dry, then touch wide end of tube 97 to center of pistil, holding it upside down. "Scrape" the tube against the pistil, using light pressure, and holding tube at a 45° angle. Stop pressure and pull away. Repeat for five petals. Hang upside down on cake rack to dry.

THE SAMPAQUITA resembles a long stem of tiny roses, starting with a bud at the tip. Fill a decorating cone, fitted with tube 59°, with yellow royal icing on one side, white on the other. Cut about 24 lengths of fine florists' wire into 10″ lengths. Work upside down as you did for daisy. At tip of wire, pipe three petals for a closed bud. At ¾″ intervals, pipe a few more buds, then add petals and turn tube outward to pipe rose-like flowers. Hook end of wire over cake rack to dry.

Form airy bouquets

You will need two small bouquets to set at the foot of the stairways, two arrangements to set between lower tiers and a larger one for the vase. Make loops from lengths of ribbon and bind with fine florists' wire. For poufs, cut tulle into 4″ squares and gather at center with wire. Now group several daisies, calachuchis, ribbon loops and poufs and twist wire stems together into a small bouquet for stairway.

For between-tiers bouquet, ice a 3″ half-ball of styrofoam and attach it to top plate of a heart ornament base. Push stems into styrofoam.

For bouquet for vase, group several small bouquets, adding sprays of sampaquita. Push a block of styrofoam into vase and insert flowers. Bend sampaquita sprays into graceful curves.

Bake and ice tiers

Each of the two large cakes consists of four round tiers, each tier two layers. Base tier is 16″ x 4″

CALACHUCHI

SAMPAQUITA SPRAY

12

high, then a 12″ x 4″ tier and a 10″ x 4″ tier. Top tier is 6″ x 3″ high. Fill and ice the tiers with buttercream, then assemble with pillars and plates as pictured.

Divide base tier into eighths, using pillars as guide, and transfer patterns. (See appendix.) Divide 12″, 10″ and 6″ tiers into fourths and transfer patterns.

Decorate the cake

Do all decorating with boiled icing.

ON BASE TIER, outline pattern curves with tube 4, adding tube 2 dots at points. Pipe bottom shell border with tube 32, then pipe a top border of curved "C"-shaped shells with same tube. Edge separator plate with tube 14.

ON 12″ TIER, cover side of tier, up to marked pattern, with "sotas", quick Philippine lace work. Pipe meandering curves and loops with tube 1, letting the sotas extend over top edge of tier to base of tier above. Outline pattern with tube 4, adding tube 2 dots at points.

ON 10″ TIER, outline side patterns with tube 4, adding tube 2 dots. Just below each design, pipe two curved shells with tube 22. Fill in rest of base border with tube 18 rosettes. Pipe a reverse shell top border with same tube.

ON TOP TIER, outline pattern with tube 3 scallops. Fill in top and sides of tier, up to scallops, with tube 1 sotas. Finish with a tube 18 shell border at base.

Trim cake with flowers

Attach a little spray of stemmed flowers to cherub fountain. Set between two upper tiers. Attach Angelinos to side of 12″ tiers with icing. Now clip stems off flowers and trim the tiers as pictured, attaching flowers with dots of icing.

ASSEMBLE STAIRWAY with bridge and trim bridge with flowers. Attach flowers to fountain frame and vase.

STAGE THE STUNNING TABLEAU on the reception table. Set the twin cakes about 14″ apart. Place fountain in center. Have a helper hold the stairway above cakes as you adjust position. Set stairway in place, then add wedding couple and bridesmaid figures. At the foot of the stairs, place the two small bouquets. Top of the World is complete—and breathtaking!

Three lower tiers of each cake serve 234 guests for a total of 468 servings. Freeze the two top tiers for a first anniversary celebration.

14

White birch

Above the lowest tier, slender white birch trees lift their branches to encircle a splashing fountain. You'll need a little skill in carpentry to create this woodland scene—or ask a friend to help you. White Birch will be the most talked-about wedding cake of the year!

ASSEMBLE YOUR ACCESSORIES

8" circle of styrofoam, 4" high
Six ⅝" dowel rods,
*   cut to 13½" length*
Two 18" plates (from
*   Arched pillar set)*
Ten stud plates
Ring pan
Kolor-flo fountain
Stiff florists' wire
Two 14" round plates
*   (from Crystal clear set)*
Six 6½" Arched pillars
Petite bridal couple
Kissing lovebirds

Prepare the separators

FOR THE UPPER SEPARATOR, use two 14" plates. Remove two pillar projections from each plate, leaving two directly opposite each other. Mark an 8" circle on plate, then glue four stud plates to plate, so you achieve six equally spaced projections for pillars. Inner edges of stud plates touch marked circle. Paint the lower plate with thinned green royal icing, dry, attach bridal couple to center, then assemble the two plates with arched pillars.

FOR THE LOWER SEPARATOR, turn lower 18" plate over so plain side, without projections, is on top. Mark a 12" circle on plate and glue on six evenly spaced stud plates, inner edges touching marked circle. On upper plate, mark a 12" circle and glue on six stud plates, inner edges touching circle—one between each pillar projection.

SUGAR MOLD THE "GRASSY BANK" that conceals motor of fountain. Use ring pan as mold. Enlarge hole in center to receive motor. Ice with green royal icing and rough up with a damp sponge. Mark a 15" circle on lower plate, ice within it with thinned green royal icing and ice sugar mold in center. Remove top level of fountain and place fountain in hole.

Set dowel rods into stud plates on lower plate. Drill three holes in each rod at an angle at front and on each side to receive "branches". Use 3/16" drill bit. Twist several lengths of stiff florists' wire together, insert in holes, tape to secure and spread ends of wires for branches. Cover "tree trunks" and branches with tube 13 lines, building up over stud plates.

Prepare the tiers

PIPE DROP FLOWERS in royal icing with tubes 190, 131 and 33. Paint base of bird ornament with thinned green icing.

BAKE, FILL AND ICE TIERS. All are two layers, for a finished height of 4"—except top tier which is 3" high.

BASE TIER: six two-layer 9" heart cakes surrounding the 8" styrofoam

Insert dowels, drill holes, insert wire "branches". Ice "trees".

circle. Ice circle with royal icing and place on a 8" circle of corrugated cardboard. Each heart is placed on its own cake board.

Tier above trees: 16" round. Tier above arched pillars: 12" round. Top tier: 8" round.

Decorate the cake

Divide each of the three upper tiers in twelfths and mark near base.

ON 16" TIER, pipe tube 18 base shell border, feathery side scrolls with tube 16, and a tube 17 reverse shell top border. Edge separator plate with tube 16.

ON 12" TIER, pipe a tube 17 base shell border, add curved scrolls and fleurs-de-lis with tube 16, tube 13 zigzag garlands at top. Drape garlands with tube 2 string and finish with a tube 16 reverse shell top border.

ON TOP TIER, pipe a tube 14 base shell border. Do curves and upright shells on side with tube 16, and finish with a tube 16 top border.

HEART CAKES ARE IDENTICAL. Pipe a tube 18 base shell border, a tube 17 top border. Add curved scrolls on top with the same tube. Spatula-stripe a decorating bag with green icing, fill with white and pipe curves on sides with tube 17.

TRIM BIRD ORNAMENT, "grassy bank" and all tiers with flowers. Add tube 65 leaves on heart cakes. Pipe "grass" around fountain and tree trunks with tube 2.

Put it all together

Assemble on the reception table. Set heart cakes in place around styrofoam circle. Position birch tree separator with fountain. Pipe leaves on the branches with a "V"-cut cone.

Drape 4" squares of white tulle casually over branches, then cover with leaves. Set upper plate with top three tiers on tree pillars, then add a few more leaves. White Birch is complete! Top tier serves 30, all other tiers serve 354.

Top view of heart cakes surrounding styrofoam circle. Circle supports weight.

Nosegay

A procession of bridesmaids and groomsmen climb lacy stairways to the top of the prettiest bridal cake of the season!

A unique angled construction of the three cakes makes Nosegay interesting from every angle. This is a large cake, serving over 350 guests, but all the details are dainty and feminine—delicate lattice, leafy trim and curving garlands. A sweet touch of color is added by the pale pink tiers. Silk flowers echo the color scheme—the arrangements will be treasured for years as mementos of the radiant wedding day.

AS A SPECIAL TOUCH, arrange a nosegay of flowers in a lacy frame. The bride will toss it to a lucky bridesmaid.

ASSEMBLE YOUR ACCESSORIES

A complete Filigree stairway set
Two Lazy daisy servers
A 14" plate and 18" footed base plate (from Tall tier stand)
Four 9" separator plates
Four 5" Corinthian pillars
Four 7" Corinthian pillars
Five 2¾" Filigree bells
Top plate from small Heart ornament base
Bridesmaid and groomsmen figures
Bridal couple figures
Silk flowers and ribbon

Please turn the page

the plate of one serving stand with the 14″ plate.

SINGLE-TIER SATELLITE is a two-layer 10″ round, 4″ high.

FILL AND ICE all tiers, then assemble with plates and pillars. Single-tier satellite rests on lazy daisy stand, two-tier satellite on stand with 14″ plate. Main cake is on 18″ footed base plate.

DIVIDE AND MARK TIERS. Divide single-tier satellite into tenths and mark midway on side. For two-tier satellite, divide base tier into tenths and mark midway on side. Divide top tier in tenths and mark 1″ up from bottom.

On main cake, divide base tier into sixteenths and mark on side, about 1¼″ from top. Divide 12″ tier into sixteenths and mark 1″ from base. Divide 8″ tier into tenths and mark 1″ up from base. Do the same for top 6″ tier.

Decorate single-tier satellite

Pipe a tube 18 shell border at base. Drop string guidelines for garlands from mark to mark, then pipe puffy tube 16 zigzag garlands. Over-pipe with a second garland. To pipe lattice, drop a string guideline to define top of lattice. Pipe with tube 2, first dropping strings in one direction, then in opposite direction. Edge lattice, top and bottom, with tube 2 beading. Drop tube 2 strings below lattice, then top each point with graduated dots.

On top of cake, pipe curved tube 16 garlands, lining them up with lattice below. Pipe a trio of tube 66 leaves between each garland, centering with a tube 3 dot.

Decorate two-tier satellite

ON BASE TIER, pipe a tube 18 bottom shell border. Drop string guidelines for garlands following marks, and leaving 1″ open space between each. Pipe tube 16 zigzag garlands, then over-pipe with a second garland for depth.

Drop string guidelines to define top of lattice, then pipe lattice with tube 2. Edge lattice with tube 2 beading, then drop strings below with same tube. Pipe a cluster of four tube 66 leaves between each lattice curve. Center with a tube 3 dot. Pipe a tube 17 top shell border and edge separator plate with tube 14 shells.

Do trims in advance

Glue a bell to top plate of heart base. Press in a half-ball of styrofoam and arrange silk flowers by inserting stems into styrofoam. Complete with a ribbon bow.

For ornament within pillars of satellite cake, join four bells by passing a fine wire through hanging loops. Add a ribbon bow and a rose. Fill the bells with poufs of pastel tulle.

Make a tiny bouquet of silk flowers and tie stems with a ribbon. This will be placed on cake at bottom of stairway. (To make sure flowers will not touch icing, set the bouquet on a small circle of clear plastic wrap.)

For nosegay, arrange flowers in a lace frame (obtain from florist). Tie stems with long streamers of ribbon. Glue a few blue flowers to the streamers. Every bride needs "something blue".

Prepare two-layer tiers

FOR MAIN CAKE you will need four round tiers—16″ x 4″, 12″ x 4″, 8″ x 3″ and 6″ x 3″.

FOR TWO-TIER SATELLITE, cake, you'll need a 12″ x 4″ round base tier and an 8″ x 3″ top tier. Replace

ON TOP TIER, bottom border hangs slightly below separator plate. To make moving the tier safe, set plate on which tier rests on a 5″ block of styrofoam, 2″ or more thick. Secure plate to block with a stroke of icing. Pipe a tube 16 base shell border. Drop string guidelines for garlands from mark to mark. Pipe garlands with tube 16 zigzags. On side of tier, above garlands, pipe a colonial scroll with the same tube, using garlands as guides for spacing. Trim with tube 65 leaves.

Pipe leafy top border with tube 66. Just pipe overlapping leaves around edge of cake. Now go back and drop double tube 2 strings over garlands at base of tier.

Decorate main cake

DO TWO LOWER TIERS as a unit, starting with 12″ tier. Edge separator plate with tube 15. Pipe top border of tube 67 overlapping leaves. Pipe a tube 17 bottom shell border. Drop string guidelines for garlands from mark to mark, then pipe zigzag garlands with tube 16. Drape with tube 2 triple strings. Above garlands, pipe curves of tube 2 dots, then add tube 67 perky leaves.

ON BASE TIER, pipe top border of tube 16 zigzag garlands. Pipe a tube 19 bottom shell border. Drop string guidelines for garlands from mark to mark, then pipe tube 16 zigzag garlands. Over-pipe with tube 16 zigzags for depth. Drop string guidelines to define top of lattice, then pipe lattice with tube 2, and edge with beading piped with same tube. Drop tube 2 strings above, then add trios of tube 66 leaves.

DO TWO TOP TIERS as a unit. Since base border on 8″ tier hangs below separator plate, set plate (with two top tiers on it) on a 5″ block of styrofoam, at least 2″ thick. Secure with a stroke of icing.

START WITH TOP TIER. Pipe a top border of tube 66 overlapping leaves. Pipe a tube 16 bottom shell border. Drop string guidelines for garlands from mark to mark, then pipe zigzag tube 16 garlands. Drop double tube 2 strings above them, then curves of dots.

ON 8″ TIER, pipe tube 16 shell borders at top and bottom. Drop string guidelines for garlands from mark to mark—then do tube 16 zigzag garlands, letting them extend to very edge of plate. Over-pipe with same tube. Drop strings to define top of lattice, then do tube 2 lattice. Edge with tube 2 beading and add vertical rows of dots at points. Pipe a tube 67 leaf between each garland, point extending beyond plate.

Put it all together on the reception table

You'll need a friend to help you arrange cakes. Consult the diagram, and place the three cakes on the table. Join upper stairway to bridge. Ask your friend to hold it over two larger cakes as you adjust positions. Set stairway and bridge in place. Hold lower stairway over two smaller cakes, adjust positions and set in place.

Add ribbon and flower trims to bases of servers. Place bell ornament within pillars of two-tier satellite cake, flower arrangement within pillars of main cake. Add flower trim to stairway. Place bridesmaids and groomsmen on stairs, bridal couple on bridge. The pretty picture is complete! As a final touch, set bouquet of flowers near cake. Nosegay will serve 362 guests. The top tier will be frozen for the first anniversary of the couple's wedding.

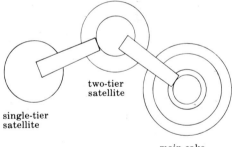

two-tier satellite

single-tier satellite

main cake

Celebration

A SPECTACULAR CENTERPIECE for life's biggest celebration! There never was a lovelier, more elaborate wedding cake. The entire bridal procession is reproduced on six lacy stairways ascending to the happy couple.

CELEBRATION is a most lavish cake, but all the trim on the main cake and its six surrounding satellites is done with only basic techniques, quickly executed. The towering main cake is handsome on its own for a smaller reception—a satellite would make a pretty shower or party cake.

ASSEMBLE YOUR ACCESSORIES
For main cake:

Twelve 5" Corinthian pillars
Six 7" Corinthian pillars
Two 16", two 10" and two 7"
  Hexagon separator plates
Six Kneeling cherub fountains
Bridge from Filigree
  stairway set
Angel fountain
Floral scroll ornament base
Two Small doves
Silk flowers and ribbon

For satellite cakes
Six Filigree stairways
Bridesmaid figures
Groomsmen figures

Please turn the page

Celebration
Continued

Prepare tiers and trim

Be sure to note sizes and heights of tiers carefully. This will ensure that the six stairways will fit properly.

FOR MAIN CAKE, bake, fill and ice two-layer tiers. Base is 16″ x 4″ round, next a 15″ x 3″ hexagon, then a 9″ x 4″ hexagon. Top tier is 6″ x 3″ round. Assemble on 20″ cake board with plates and pillars. Note that 7″ pillars go above 15″ hexagon tier.

Divide base tier into sixths, using pillars as guides, and mark near bottom. Divide these spaces into thirds and mark midway on side. Divide each side of 15″ hexagon tier into thirds and mark midway on sides. On 9″ hexagon tier, divide each side into thirds and mark 1″ up from base. On top tier, divide in sixths and mark midway on side.

FOR SIX SATELLITE CAKES, bake, fill and ice two-layer 12″ hexagon cakes. Each cake should be 4″ high. Set on 14″ cake boards cut in hexagon shape. Starting 1″ in from each corner, divide into fourths and mark 1″ up from base. Lightly press a 9″ hexagon pan on top of each cake to make guide for scallop trim.

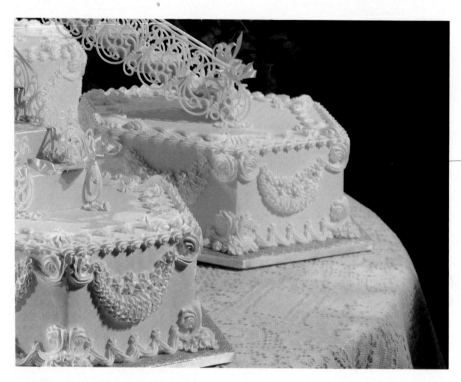

PIPE DROP FLOWERS in royal icing with tubes 224, 225 and 131.

TURN LOWER PART of ornament base upside down and secure to top plate. Fill "bowl" with styrofoam. Arrange bouquet by sticking stems of silk flowers into styrofoam. Glue fine wire to doves and insert into bouquet.

Decorate identical satellites

Pipe a tube 19 curved shell at each corner of base of cake. Fill in rest of bottom border with tube 17 shells. Drop tube 16 strings from mark to mark over shells and top with stars. Pipe a tube 19 curved shell at each corner, starting at top edge of cake. Drop guidelines, then pipe tube 17 zigzag garlands. Pipe a tube 17 top shell border. On top of cake, pipe tube 19 fleurs-de-lis, extending in from each corner. Following marked pattern, pipe tube 16 scallops and stars. Attach drop flowers within garlands and at lower corners of cake.

Decorate main cake

ON BASE TIER, pull up a tube 4B pillar from each mark. Fill in bottom border and do top border with tube 19 shells. Use the same tube to pipe fleurs-de-lis and stars on top of piped pillars. Then pipe three curved shells on side of tier to connect pillars. Edge separator plate with tube 16 shells.

ON 15″ HEXAGON TIER, pull up a tube 22 pillar on each corner. Fill in with a tube 19 bottom shell border. Pipe curved tube 19 shells from top of each piped pillar on side of tier to form scallop effect. For top border, pipe a thick line of icing on edge of tier and press in drop flowers.

TWO TOP TIERS will be assembled with two lower tiers on the reception table. Do not attach 10″ separator plate to 15″ hexagon tier at this time. (This will make it easier to attach stairways to cakes on the reception table.)

ON 9″ HEXAGON TIER, pipe base border with tube 16 shells. Use same tube for dropped string and stars. Pipe a curved shell from each corner at top of tier, then drop guidelines and pipe garlands with tube 16. Cover garlands with drop flowers. Do top border with tube 17 rosettes. Edge separator plate with tube 14 shells.

ON TOP TIER, do all decorating with

tube 16. Pipe a bottom shell border, then drop guidelines and pipe garlands from mark to mark. Mark curves to connect garlands and attach flowers in scallop effect. Pipe a reverse shell top border.

Put everything together

On the reception table, place assembled *two lower tiers only* of main cake, making sure it is centered on table.

Now arrange satellite cakes. Set each about 1″ away from main cake, lining up inner edges carefully with pillars on main cake.

Ask a friend to help you set the stairways in position. Tops will rest on 15″ hexagon tier, bases on satellite cakes. Trim bases with a few drop flowers and ribbon bows. Now assemble top two tiers of main cake with pillars. Secure 10″ separator plate on 15″ hexagon tier. Edge with tube 16 shells. Set bridge within 7″ pillars, pose couple on bridge. Arrange silk flowers in a garland around bridge. Set silk flower bouquet on top of main cake. Form the bridal procession by posing groomsmen and bridesmaids on stairways. Stand back to admire the breathtaking effect!

Omitting the top tier, Celebration will serve 654 guests.

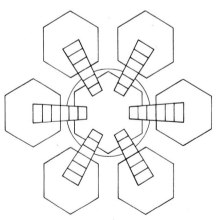

Arrange six satellite cakes around two lower tiers of main cake. Attach six stairways, then add two top tiers of main cake.

Wedding March

Pretty as a picture with lots of feminine, lacy appeal! Three shallow square tiers at the base are perfect for showing off pretty bridesmaid figures. Pose this large, lovely cake in the center of the reception room so it can be admired from all sides.

ASSEMBLE YOUR ACCESSORIES
Two 11" Clear plates
Four 5" Clear pillars
Clear ornament
Bride and groom figures
Bridesmaid figures
16 Flower spikes
Silk flowers

Bake and ice the tiers

FOR SQUARE BASE TIER you will need four single-layer 12" square cakes, set on a 24" square cake board. Square tier above is made up of four single-layer 10" square cakes on a 20" cake board. Third tier is a single-layer 16" square on a 16" cake board. Make sure all square tiers are 2" high.

Lowest round tier is 14", two layers, 4" high. Next a two-layer 10" round, 4" high. At the top, a two-layer 8" round, 3" high.

Fill and ice all tiers, then assemble with plates and pillars. Use a 27" square cake board at base, trimmed with a ruffle. Be sure to insert dowels in all tiers (Chapter Nine). except top tier. This a large, heavy cake! Buttercream is recommended for covering the tiers. Boiled icing is best for all the lacy trim.

Transfer patterns to all tiers.

Decorate the cake

Decorate the assembled four lower tiers as a unit and the assembled two round upper tiers as a unit. *Work from top down* on both units.

DECORATE LOWER TIERS. Make a recipe of rolled fondant (Chapter Nine), tint and roll out to about ¼" thickness or less. Cut out "stairway carpets" and smooth over three square tiers, trimming as necessary where carpets touch 14" round tier. Cut out scallop pattern for 14" round tier and smooth to tier at base. Using a 6" pan or cake circle as pattern, cut out a circle of fondant and center on lower separator plate. Edge with a tube 5 ball border.

On round 14" tier, cover scalloped fondant area with tube 1 "sotas"—meandering curves and loops of boiled icing. Edge scallops with tube 3 beading, then add fleurs-de-lis at points. Pipe tube 7 ball borders around separator plate and at top and bottom edges of tier.

On three square tiers, edge carpet with tube 3 beading, then add scallops with same tube. Fill in marked areas with tube 1 sotas, bringing it up to bases of tiers above.

Pipe tube 3 beading around sotas.

Pipe tube 5 ball borders up to carpet areas as shown in picture. Pipe a tube 7 ball border at base.

DECORATE TWO UPPER TIERS. Fill in marked, scalloped areas with tube 1 sotas, starting with top tier. Carry sotas over top edge of 10" tier as pictured. Edge scallops on top tier with tube 2 "e" motion loops. Edge scallops on 10" tier with tube 2 beading, then tiny scallops. Finish top edge of top tier with a tube 5 ball border. Pipe a tube 6 ball border at base of 10" tier.

Put it all together

Transport the two units of the cake separately to the reception table, then assemble with pillars. Set ornament on top. Place clusters of flowers at base of each pillar, then add figures of couple. Insert flower spikes near carpet on 20" and 24" square tiers. Fill with flower clusters. Pose bridesmaid figures on "stairs". Wedding March is a rosy vision!

When serving the cake, cut the three square tiers into 2" wide slices instead of the customary 1" slices. (These tiers are single layers.) Wedding March will serve 448, not counting the top tier.

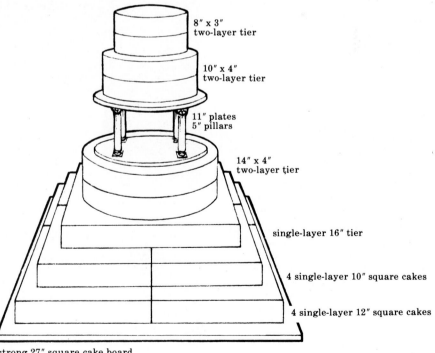

8" x 3" two-layer tier

10" x 4" two-layer tier

11" plates 5" pillars

14" x 4" two-layer tier

single-layer 16" tier

4 single-layer 10" square cakes

4 single-layer 12" square cakes

strong 27" square cake board

Natural Beauty

This dainty flounced confection is set off by a rainbow of silk flowers. Despite its size, Natural Beauty has a quaint Victorian charm. The little bouquets within pillars of the satellite cakes are gifts for the mothers of the couple.

ASSEMBLE YOUR ACCESSORIES

For main cake you'll need:
A complete Stairway set
Four 7" Corinthian pillars
Two 10" plates
Petite ornament
Bridal couple figures
Bridesmaid figures

For two satellite cakes:
Eight 7" Corinthian pillars
Four 8" plates
Two 2" Filigree bells
*Two top plates from
   small Heart bases*

Bake and ice the tiers

FOR MAIN CAKE you'll need 16", 12", 10" and 6" round two-layer tiers. Layers for 16" and 10" tiers are 2" high for a finished height of 4"—12" and 6" tiers are 3" high. Fill, ice and assemble the tiers with pillars.

Divide base tier into eighths and mark about 1½" below top edge. Make a second series of marks 2" away from first marks. Divide 12" tier into sixteenths and mark about 1" down from top. Divide 10" tier into twelfths, marking midway on side. Divide top edge of 6" tier into eighths and mark.

EACH OF THE TWO SIDE CAKES consists of a base two-layer tier 12" square, 4" high—and an 8" two-layer top tier, 3" high. Fill, ice and assemble.

On base tiers, mark each side 1" in from corner, about 1½" from bottom. Divide and mark remaining space into fifths. On top of tier, measure 1½" in from each corner, then divide remaining space in thirds. Mark about 1½" in from edge. Divide top tier into eighths and mark midway on side.

Please turn the page

Prepare trims in advance

Make vases for bouquets by gluing a bell to a small heart base, then wedging in a half-ball of styrofoam. Arrange flowers. Arrange an arch of flowers at back of stairway bridge to frame couple. Make two small bouquets for base of stairs.

Pipe white sweet peas in royal icing and tube 104.

Decorate the cake

ON MAIN CAKE, pipe a tube 19 bottom shell border on base tier. Drape a curved tube 16 zigzag garland from mark to mark on side of tier, first a small curve, then a large. Cover with a tube 104 ruffle. Top each point with a tube 14 rosette. Pipe a tube 17 top shell border, then a tube 104 ruffle to circle the edge.

ON 12″ TIER, pipe a tube 17 shell border, then pipe curved zigzag garlands from mark to mark with tube 16. Attach sweet peas at points. Pipe a fluffy sweet pea top border with tube 104. First pipe a sweet pea on top of tier, then another one, just below it, on side of tier. Continue piping sweet peas, first on top, then on side. Edge separator plate with tube 15.

ON 10″ TIER, pipe a tube 16 base shell border. Then pipe zigzag tube 16 garlands from mark to mark, allowing garlands to extend slightly below base of cake. Top with tube 104 ruffles, then tube 15 rosettes at points. Attach a trio of sweet peas between each garland, extending below base of tier. To pipe "hanging" borders like this, set the tier on a block of styrofoam at least 2″ smaller in diameter than the tier. Pipe puffy tube 16 garlands at top edge.

ON 6″ TIER, pipe tube 16 shell borders at bottom and top. Pipe a tube 104 ruffle over shells at base, then curved ruffles on side of tier with the same tube.

SATELLITE CAKES ARE IDENTICAL. Pipe a tube 17 shell border at bottom of base tier, then pipe curved garlands with tube 16. Top points with sweet peas, then pipe curved ruffles from mark to mark on top of tier. Pipe a tube 16 top shell border. Edge separator plate with tube 15. On top tier, pipe a tube 16 shell border at base. Top with tube 16 "hanging" garlands,

similar to garlands on 10″ tier of main cake. Add fleurs-de-lis, then attach sweet peas between garlands at base. Pipe a tube 16 shell border at top of tier, then a tube 104 ruffle.

Put it all together

On the reception table, set the three cakes in a row, cake boards touching. Put assembled stairway in position, then place bridal couple and bridesmaids. Set ornament and bouquets within pillars—small bouquets at base of stairway. Natural Beauty is as sweet as the bride! Omitting top tier, it will serve 438 guests.

Queen of Hearts

At right: an exquisite, towering showpiece! Six heart-shaped cakes beneath arched pillars surround a sparkling fountain.

ASSEMBLE ACCESSORIES
Arched pillar set
Kolor-flo fountain
Seven Kneeling cherub fountains
Ten Cherub card holders
Two 10″ separator plates
Four 5″ Grecian pillars
Ten 2″ filigree bells
Top ornament

Pipe flowers, bake tiers

PIPE WHITE ROSES with tube 104 and royal icing. Set aside to dry.

BAKE SIX 9″ HEART CAKES, each two layers for a height of 4″. For main cake, bake two-layer tiers, 16″, 12″ and 8″, each 4″ high. Fill and ice with buttercream and assemble. Divide 8″ tier into 16ths, 12″ tier into 10ths and 16″ tier into 10ths. Mark at top edges. Mount heart cakes on foil-covered cake boards.

Decorate the cake

HEART CAKES ARE IDENTICAL. Make double heart pattern for top of cake. Outline pattern with a circular motion of tube 15. Pipe base reverse shell border with tube 74. At top edge pipe zigzag garlands with tube 15, then trim with tube 3 stringwork.

ON 16″ TIER, pipe curved shell border at base with tube 32. Drop string guidelines for garlands from top edge, leaving 1″ space between each. Pipe zigzag garlands with tube 17, and drop triple strings with tube 4. Pipe reverse shell top border with tube 75.

ON 12″ TIER, pipe reverse shell base border with tube 20. Drop string guidelines for garlands, leaving ½″ space between each. Pipe garlands with tube 15 and drop double strings with tube 4. Pipe top shell border with tube 17.

ON TOP TIER, pipe vertical rows of tube 14 shells, starting at marks. Between rows, pipe curving tube 3 stems, then add tube 81 lilies of the valley. Edge top and bottom with tube 14 garlands.

ADD TRIMS. Attach bells between garlands on 16″ tier. Trim all tiers with roses. At the reception table, assemble all tiers with pillars and place cherub figures and ornament. Circle the main cake with the six heart cakes. Queen of Hearts is beautiful! Omitting top tier, it will serve 354 guests.

Queen of Hearts

Cloud Nine

A cake for a very large reception with a dainty personality and fresh young charm! Prim little drop flowers add a rosy touch and create a delightful border. Curving stairways lead to the bridal couple.

ASSEMBLE YOUR ACCESSORIES

Two 18" plates from Arched pillar set
Six 7" Corinthian pillars
Two 9" plates
Four 5" Corinthian pillars
Two sets of Musical trio cherubs
Two top plates from small Heart bases
4" Filigree heart
Three Old-fashioned fence sets
Stairstep set
Bride and groom figures
Seed pearl heart
Top plate from Heart base

Do trims in advance

PIPE DROP FLOWERS. Tint royal icing in two shades of pink and use tubes 131, 135 and 96. Add tube 2 yellow centers to all flowers.

PREPARE ORNAMENTS. For ornament between two lower tiers, first make a 10" pink circular base. Cut from gum paste, using a cake circle as pattern, or use the Color Flow method. Attach to center of 18" plate and border with tube 2 beading. Secure fence to base with royal icing, leaving front opening.

Glue a filigree heart to top plate of small heart base, then glue two cherub figures in front of it. Trim with flowers and a satin bow.

For ornament between two upper tiers, attach a pink tulle ruffle to under side of a small plate. Glue three cherub figures to plate, then trim with flowers.

For top ornament, cut pink tulle in 4" squares. Bunch each square at center and push through openings in seed pearl heart. Glue heart to ornament base, and trim with drop flowers. Add bridal couple.

DROP OVERLAPPING STRING

ADD FLOWERS, THEN LEAVES

Bake and ice the tiers

All tiers are two layers. Base tier consists of four 10" x 4" square cakes put together to form a 20" tier. Mount on a 24" cake board, covered with foil and ruffle trimmed. Second tier is a 16" x 4" round. Tier above is 12" x 4". Top tier is 8" round, 3" high.

Fill and ice all tiers with buttercream and assemble with plates and pillars as shown.

Decorate the cake

Use boiled icing for all trim.

ON BASE TIER, measure 3" in from each corner and mark on all sides of tier at top edge. Divide remaining spaces in fourths and mark at top edges. Pipe a tube 4B bottom shell border. With the same tube, pipe a garland at each corner of tier from mark to mark, dropping down almost to base. Pipe four shallower garlands in spaces between corner garlands. Add tube 4 double string drape and loops. Finish with a tube 32 top shell border. Edge separator plate with tube 501.

ON 16" TIER, divide into 20ths and mark sides 1½" down from top edge. Make a second series of marks ½" away from first marks. Pipe overlapping tube 4 strings from mark to mark. Finish with trios of drop flowers and tube 65 leaves. Pipe base shell border and reverse shell top border with tube 504.

ON 12" TIER, lightly mark a triangle on front and back of the side—6" wide at top, 3" deep. Pipe a tube 504 base shell border. Outline marked triangle with curved "C"-shaped shells using tube 502. Pipe a tube 504 top shell border. Edge separator plate with tube 501.

ON TOP TIER, divide into 10ths and mark on top edge. Use tube 504 to pipe a curved shell base border. Drop triple tube 3 strings from mark to mark and add loops. Do top shell border with tube 504.

Add final touches

First attach stairways. Snap twelve steps together for each stairway. Starting about 3½" from center front of 12" tier, push pegs through four steps into side of tier, curving to back. Let five steps hang in space. Continue at back of 8" tier, pushing pegs through three steps into side of tier. Ask a helper to hold the steps as you push pegs into tiers. Repeat on other side of cake for double stairway. Secure fence to projecting pegs on stairs with royal icing. Attach flowers to fence and stairs with royal icing.

Attach flowers to 12" and base tiers as pictured. Trim with tube 65 leaves. When the cake is placed on the reception table, put the prepared ornaments in position. One look, and the bride will be on Cloud Nine! Three lower tiers serve 386 guests.

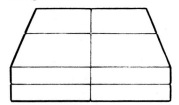

Base tier consists of
four two-layer 10" square cakes.

Morning Glory

An appropriate centerpiece for the glorious celebration! The many tiers are enriched by interesting borders and softened by clusters and twining vines of rosy flowers. Walk around Morning Glory—it's beautiful from any angle.

ASSEMBLE YOUR ACCESSORIES
For satellite cake:

Two 11" round separator plates
Four 7" Corinthian pillars
Petite ornament

For main cake:

Two 13" round separator plates
Two 7" square separator plates
Four 10¼" Roman columns
Four 5" Grecian pillars
Petite and regular-sized ornaments (remove lower base from petite ornament)
Filigree Stairway and Bridge
Curved gothic window
Bridal couple figures
Bridesmaid figures

Pipe the flowers

Pipe the morning glories in royal icing and 1⅝" lily nail, lined with foil. Coil a tube 104 band of icing within well of nail. Change to tube 103 and pipe outer edge, increasing pressure in five places to form angular shape. Brush flower smooth and dry. Add tube 1 white lines and center dot. Pipe sepals on back with tube 33. For smaller flowers, change to a 1¼" nail and tubes 102 and 103. For tiniest blossoms, use a 1¼" nail and tubes 101 and 102. Pipe spikes on backs of 16 of middle-sized flowers.

Prepare the two-layer tiers

FOR SATELLITE CAKES, bake, fill and ice a 12" x 4" square tier and 10" x 3" round tier. Assemble on 14" cake board with plates and pillars. Divide each side of base into sixths, starting 1" in from each corner. Mark 1" up from bottom. Divide top tier into sixteenths and mark midway on side.

FOR MAIN CAKE, the base tier is a 24" x 4" square. Prepare this by assembling four two-layer 12" cakes on a 24" cardboard base. Next tier is 14" x 4" square—then a 12" x 4"

Please turn the page

32

round tier. Top tier, 6″ x 3″ square.

Assemble tiers with plates and pillars on a 28″ cake board. Starting 1½″ in from each corner, divide

base tier into sevenths and mark 1½″ up from bottom. On 14″ tier, mark a 6″ diameter half-circle at center of each side. On 12″ round tier, divide into sixteenths and mark on side, 1″ up from base. On top tier, divide each side into fourths, starting 1″ in from each corner. Mark 1″ above bottom.

Decorate satellite cake

ON BASE TIER, pipe a tube 96 bottom shell border. Top with tube 77 zigzag ruffly garlands. Pipe a curving tube 3 vine and tube 3 branches around sides of tier. Trim with tube 68 leaves. Pipe shell motion top border with tube 68. Edge plate with tube 14 shells.

ON TOP TIER, pipe a tube 96 shell border at top and bottom. Following marks, pipe a deeply curved tube 3 vine and stems around side of tier. Trim with tube 68 leaves. Push spiked flowers into curves of vine on mounds of icing.

Decorate main cake

DO TWO LOWER TIERS, as a unit. On 14″ tier, pipe a tube 96 shell border at bottom, a tube 68 shell motion border at top. Outline half-circle with tube 78 curved shells. Edge

separator plate with tube 14. On base tier, pipe tube 96 shells at bottom and top. Do tube 78 garlands.

DECORATE 12″ ROUND TIER same as base tier on satellite cake. Edge separator plate with tube 14.

ON TOP TIER, pipe base border with tube 16 shells, then pipe tube 52 zigzag garlands from mark to mark. Drop tube 13 strings from top edge and add tube 68 leaves. Pipe a tube 16 top shell border.

TRIM BOTH CAKES with flowers. Make a garland of morning glories around lower separator plate. Trim ornaments with smallest flowers, then add tube 68 leaves to all flowers.

Put it all together . . .

on the reception table. Set satellite cake near main cake and attach stairway. Secure Gothic window to bridge, set on top of cake and add couple and flowers. Trim top and bottom of stairway with flowers. Finally set ornaments in place, then bridesmaid figures. Just glorious! Omitting top tier, Morning Glory will serve 592.

Lady Windemere
shown at right

Whimsical cherubs and curves of golden flowers soften the design of this gracious cake.

ASSEMBLE YOUR ACCESSORIES
 Harvest cherub separator set
 Frolicking cherub
 Four large angel figures
 Top ornament
 Round styrofoam dummy,
  6″ x 4″ high

PIPE ROYAL ICING ROSES and buds with tubes 124 and 104. Pipe daisies with tube 102, add tube 4 centers.

MAKE CAKE BOARD from three layers of corrugated cardboard (this is a heavy cake). For pattern, arrange four 14″ cake circles, sides touching. Trace around them, then draw a line 2″ beyond tracing. Tape boards together, cover with foil.

Prepare two-layer tiers

Base tier is made up of four 12″ round cakes, each 4″ high. Middle tier is 14″ x 4″, top tier 8″ x 3″. Fill

and ice all tiers.

Construct tiers as diagram shows. Center four 12″ tiers with the styrofoam dummy (this will help support tiers above). Insert dowel rods into 12″ cakes for further support. Complete construction of cake.

Divide each 12″ cake into tenths, mark at top edge. Transfer pattern to tops of cakes. Divide 14″ tier into sixteenths and mark at top edge. Mark scallops on top of tier with a cutter.

Decorate the cake

DO TWO LOWER TIERS as a unit, starting with 14″ tier. Drop string guidelines, then pipe zigzag garlands with tube 73. Pipe a ruffled leaf between each with same tube. Trim with triple tube 3 string. Pipe scallops on top of tier and edge separator plate with tube 4, using circular motion. Pipe reverse shell top border with tube 17. For bottom border, pipe tube 22 stars and trim with tube 3 string.

ON FOUR-CAKE BASE TIER, outline top patterns with tube 2 and a circular

motion. Drop string guidelines and pipe garlands with zigzags of tube 73, ruffled leaves between them with same tube. Trim with double tube 3 string. Do top shell border with tube 21 and trim with tube 3 string piped in "S" curves. Pipe reverse shell base borders with tube 32.

ON TOP TIER, circle base with tube 21 upright shells. Trim with interlaced tube 3 strings. Pipe a tube 16 star border at top.

Complete the cake with flowers

Set cherub within pillars and ornament on top. Attach angels to cake board with icing. Now trim with circles and arcs of flowers. Add tube 65 leaves. Serve two lower tiers of Lady Windemere to 364.

Top view of base tier on cake board. Tiny circles indicate dowel rods. Small center circle is styrofoam dummy.

Carillon

A SLENDER, SNOW WHITE tower of a cake, set off by two smaller confections. All the tiers are trimmed with dainty filigree bells to ring in years of happiness.

ASSEMBLE YOUR ACCESSORIES

Filigree bells: two 1", 17 of 2" size, six 2¾", two 3", one 4¼"

Three top plates (from small Heart base)

Twelve Winged angels

Three Cherub card holders

Crystal clear cake divider set with 16", 14" 12" and 10" plates and twelve twist legs (for main cake)

Two 14" and two 10" plates and eight twist legs from Crystal clear set (for satellite cakes)

Silk flowers and ribbon

Make top ornaments

FOR MAIN CAKE glue the 4¼" bell to ornament plate. Fill the bell with a styrofoam ball. Secure cherub card holder to top of ball, then ring the figure with flowers. Glue 1" bells and bows to cherub's hands.

FOR SATELLITE CAKES, make ornaments the same way, but use 3" bells. Omit tiny bells in cherubs' hands.

Prepare the two-layer tiers

FOR MAIN CAKE you will need 14", 12", 10", 8" and 6" round tiers. Three lower tiers are 4" high, two top tiers 3" high. Bake, fill and ice. Set base tier on 16" plate.

Transfer patterns to tops of tiers. Divide base tier into fourths and mark at top edge. Within these spaces, mark midway on side, 3" away from first marks. Divide 10"

and 12" tiers into eighths and mark midway on sides. For heart design on 12" tier, use a 2" cookie cutter as pattern press. On 8" tier, mark center front and back of side, 1" below top edge. Mark again, 4" away from first marks. Divide top tier into eighths and mark at top edge.

FOR IDENTICAL SATELLITES, you will need two 12" x 4" two-layer round base tiers and two 8" x 3" two-layer top tiers. Divide and mark base tier exactly like 12" tier of main cake. Divide top tiers into eighths, mark at top edge. Transfer top pattern. Set base tiers on 14" plates.

Decorate the cake

FOR SATELLITE CAKES, pipe tube 18 shell borders at bottom of 12" tiers. Drop string guidelines from mark to mark, then pipe tube 104 curving ruffles. Define heart designs with tube 17 curved shells. Outline top pattern with tube 14 curved shells. Pipe a tube 18 top shell border. then a tube 104 ruffle.

On top tiers, pipe tube 16 reverse shell borders at bottom. Drop string guidelines from mark to mark and pipe tube 104 ruffles. Top with tube 16 zigzag garlands. Outline scallop patterns with tube 14. Pipe tube 16 reverse shell top borders.

FOR MAIN CAKE, pipe a tube 9 line around bottom of base tier. Pipe a tube 125 ruffle over line. Drop string guidelines from mark to mark as guides for tube 125 ruffles. Top with tube 18 zigzag garlands, tube 28 hearts and tube 2 bows. Outline pattern on tier top with tube 14 curved shells. Pipe a tube 18 top shell border, then a tube 104 ruffle.

Decorate 12" tier exactly like base tiers on satellite cakes.

On 10" tier, pipe a tube 16 bottom shell border. Drop guidelines from

mark to mark and pipe tube 104 ruffles. Add tube 28 hearts and tube 2 bows. Outline scallops on tier top with tube 14 curved shells. Pipe a tube 16 top shell border, then a tube 104 ruffle.

Do two upper tiers as a unit. On 6" tier, pipe a tube 9 line around base and cover with a tube 104 ruffle. Drop guidelines, then pipe tube 16 zigzag garlands. Pipe a tube 16 top shell border, then a tube 104 ruffle.

On 8" tier, pipe a tube 16 bottom shell border. Drop guidelines from mark to mark and pipe tube 104 ruffles. Add tube 28 hearts. Pipe a tube 16 reverse shell top border.

Add final trims

ON MAIN CAKE, insert nylon thread through loop in 2" bell. Tape thread to underside of 10" plate and trim bell with ribbon bow. Glue winged angels to separator legs. Wire pairs of 2" bells to legs above 12" tier and trim with ribbon bows. Tape four 2¾" bells to underside of 14" plate, trim with ribbon. Attach pairs of 2" bells to base tier with icing.

ON SATELLITE CAKES, hang ribbon-trimmed 2¾" bells from underside of separator plate. Glue winged angels to legs. Set flowery ornaments on top tiers of all cakes.

TWIST THREE LENGTHS of ribbon together. Secure one end to top ornament of main cake. Glue other end to cherub's hand on satellite cake ornament. Repeat to join main cake to second satellite cake. Carillon serves 434 guests. Freeze the top tier for the first anniversary.

CHAPTER TWO

The Sweetest Cakes are trimmed with flowers

ALL THE LOVELY CAKES in this chapter are planned to serve from 110 to 250 guests—and all are adorned with flowers. Flowers can carry out the color scheme of the wedding party, repeat the bride's bouquet, or even suggest the season.

THE TYPE OF FLOWER TRIM is yours to choose—whether skillfully piped, fashioned of gum paste or silk, or nature's own. Just be sure not to use more than one type of flower trim on a cake. If you decide on silk flowers, use silk flowers only—do not mingle them with piped flowers.

FRESH FLOWERS are always exquisite. Arrange them in small vases or in flower spikes—then let your piped borders and trim set them off to their best advantage.

FLOWERS PIPED IN ROYAL ICING might be your first choice. Their crisp delicate details complete the hand-fashioned look of the beautiful cake. Almost any flower can be piped in royal icing! They may be piped weeks ahead, then quickly arranged on the cake on decorating day. They're long lasting—arrangements or even lovely single blooms may be given to guests as mementos. And only flowers piped in royal icing can be mounted on wire stems to form bouquets and sprays.

BUTTERCREAM FLOWERS are lovely, but not as versatile as royal icing flowers. Use them for simple arrangements on top of tiers. They can be piped ahead of time too—either freeze them and arrange on the cake at the last moment, or allow them to air dry for use in a few days. *Do not* decorate with buttercream flowers if the weather is hot and humid.

GUM PASTE FLOWERS are unbelievably realistic! Just like fine porcelain, with care, a gum-paste flower arrangement may be treasured for years. In this chapter you'll see an outstanding cake trimmed with golden tulips.

SILK FLOWERS make fashionable and pretty cake trims. They're time-saving, too! Arrange them just as you would fresh flowers—but keep them for years.

Filigree

At right: an airy, lacy tower of a cake with silk flowers the featured trim. Filigree is an impressive cake—but one you can decorate very quickly.

ASSEMBLE YOUR ACCESSORIES
Two 11″ square plates
Four 10″ Roman pillars
Two 9″ square plates
Four 5″ Grecian pillars
Eight Filigree pillar trims
Sixteen Filigree swirls
Garden gazebo dome
Bridal couple figures
Heart bowl vase
Four Flower spikes
Petite ornament
Silk flowers

Prepare trims in advance
ARRANGE BOUQUET in bowl. Secure a 3″ half-ball of styrofoam in bowl with royal icing. Arrange the flowers by pushing stems into styrofoam. For a dainty touch, bunch 4″ squares of tulle and bind with florists' wire. Add these poufs to the bouquet. Make four small clusters for corners of cake. Trim ornament and dome with flowers.

Bake and ice the tiers
All the square tiers are two layers for a finished height of 4″. Base tier is 18″ x 4″. Diagram shows construction of base tier. Assemble with pillars and plates and mount on a 22″ foil-covered cake board.

On base tier, measure 3″ in from each corner and mark at top edge. Lightly mark three 4″ half-circles on sides and top of tier. (A cooky cutter does this quickly.) Mark center of top edge on all sides of other two tiers.

Decorate the cake
ON BASE TIER, outline marked half-circles with tube 16 scallops. Top points with tube 13 stars. Pipe tube 18 fleurs-de-lis between half-circles on sides of tier. Pipe a tube 18 rosette border at bottom, a tube 16 shell border at top. Edge separator plate with tube 16.

ON MIDDLE TIER, pipe a tube 16 free-hand design on each side. Pipe shell borders with same tube. Edge separator plate with tube 14.

ON TOP TIER, pipe tube 16 free-hand designs and shell borders.

Put it all together
Attach a filigree pillar trim to each corner of the base tier by piping mounds of icing on sides. Attach filigree swirls to corners of two upper tiers the same way. Snap pillar trims to 5″ pillars.

Place the cake on the reception table. Set dome and bridal couple on top, ornament within 5″ pillars. Place bouquet within 10″ pillars. Insert flower spikes into base tier near each corner. Add small flower clusters. Your beautiful cake is complete! Two lower tiers of Filigree serve 212.

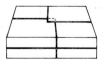

Base tier is made up of two 8″ square cakes and two 10″ cakes. Cut out square in center as shown.

Rose Bouquet

Here's a new idea for the wedding celebration—a petite heart-shaped cake for the parents of the bride and one for the parents of the groom are set beside the wedding cake.

ASSEMBLE YOUR ACCESSORIES
For the bride's cake:
  Four Twist legs
  One 6" plate
  (from Crystal clear set)
  Bridal couple figures
  Angelino
  Two Cherub card holders
  Four Flower spikes
For the parents' cakes:
  Heart mini-tier pan sets
  Two small Cherub figures

Decorate the wedding cake

This most feminine of pale pink cakes is lavished with bouquets and sprays of pastel flowers. Piped baby's breath makes the flower arrangements especially airy.

PIPE ROYAL ICING FLOWERS. The baby's breath is quick and easy to achieve. Twist ten or twelve lengths of fine florists' wire into a sprig. Pull out many tube 1 points on the end of each wire. Push sprig into styrofoam to dry. Make tube 101s forget-me-nots and pipe roses with tubes 103 and 104. Mount on wire stems. Pipe leaves directly on wires with tube 66.

Make a bouquet for top of cake and tie with ribbons. Arrange two smaller bouquets to flank the bridal couple figures. Make two clusters and two sprays to trim base tier and a third cluster to set below Angelino. Arrange a tiny spray to place in hands of one cherub.

BAKE, FILL AND ICE THE TIERS —14" square, 10" round and 6" round. All are two layers. Assemble on a ruffle-edged, foil-covered board. Insert dowel rods, clipped off level with cake top, into 14" tier to support 10" tier. Elevate 6" tier with plate and pillars.

Mark a half-circle, 7" in diameter, at center front of base tier. Mark four evenly spaced 3" half-

Please turn the page

circles on side of 10" round tier.

ON 14" TIER, pipe a tube 16 bottom shell border. With tube 17, outline marked half-circle with curved shell scallops. Pipe scallops over bottom border. Pipe a tube 16 top shell border, leaving half-circle open. Polka-dot sides with tube 13.

ON 10" TIER, pipe a tube 16 bottom shell border. Pipe tube 17 curved shell scallops over bottom border. Outline marked half-circles with scallops. Pipe a tube 15 shell border at top of tier, leaving half-circles open. Polka-dot sides with tube 13 stars.

DO TOP TIER similar to others. Pipe tube 15 shells and curves at base, tube 15 shells at top. Stars on sides are tube 13.

Add final trims

Place large bouquet on top tier. Place bridal couple between pillars and flower clusters on either side. Attach angelino to base tier with icing. Set two cherubs on bottom tier. Place ends of ribbon in hands of one and small spray in hands of other. Push in two flower spikes at side of each cherub and insert clusters and sprays. Set another small cluster beneath angelino. Two lower tiers of Rose Bouquet serve 146 guests.

Decorate the parents' cakes

These delightful little cakes are decorated in a similar manner to the bride's cake.

PIPE ROYAL ICING FLOWERS. Pipe the baby's breath as described for wedding cake. Pipe roses and buds with tubes 101 and 102, forget-me-nots with tube 101s. Mount these flowers on wire stems. Pipe leaves on wires with tube 65. Form two bouquets for tops of tiers and tie with ribbons. Form two small sprays to place within pillars.

BAKE AND ICE THE TIERS. Bake the single-layer tiers in mini-tier pans. Ice each tier separately, then assemble two lower tiers on a ruffle-trimmed cake board. Set top tier on top plate.

DECORATE THE CAKES. Pipe a tube 15 shell border at bases of two lower tiers, a tube 14 border at top edges. Use tube 15 to pipe curved shell scallops over base borders. At points of tiers, pipe fleurs-de-lis.

On top tier pipe a tube 14 bottom shell border, tube 13 border at top edge. Pipe curved shell scallops over base border and a fleur-de-lis at point with tube 14.

Polka-dot sides of all tiers with tube 13. Place flower spray on middle tier, then assemble with pillars. Set cupids in position and crown each cake with a bouquet. Each little cake slices into twelve dessert-size servings.

Ruffled Petunia

At right: a pure white, classically beautiful cake softened with beautifully piped petunias.

ASSEMBLE YOUR ACCESSORIES
Two 12" separator plates
Four 7" Corinthian pillars
Kissing lovebirds ornament
Flower spike

Pipe flowers in advance

These showy blooms are fun to pipe in royal icing. You will need about 65. Make them well in advance, then decorating the cake will be quick and easy. Line a 1⅝" two-piece lily nail with foil, then, with the narrow end of tube 102 up, start piping royal icing deep inside nail. Move up to outer edge as you turn nail, jiggling hand slightly for ruffled petals, then return to starting point. Repeat for a total of five petals. Dry, then paint the inner throat of each flower with thinned yellow icing. Pipe a tube 14 green star in center and insert a few artificial stamens.

Pipe a tube 6 royal icing spike on backs of eight flowers. Mount a dozen flowers on wire stems for bouquet on top of cake. Pipe about a dozen tube 69 leaves on wires.

Bake and ice the tiers

Bake 16" x 4", 12" x 4" and 8" x 3" two-layer round tiers. Fill, ice and insert supporting dowel rods in two lower tiers. Assemble on a strong 20" foil-covered cake board with plates and pillars.

On 16" tier, mark four 4" spaces midway on side, using pillars as guides. Divide remaining spaces into fourths and mark. On 12" tier, divide side into twelfths and mark midway on side. On top tier, divide top edge into eighths and mark.

Decorate the cake

ON BASE TIER, pipe tube 22 bottom shell border and tube 20 top shell border. Drop string guidelines for garlands, four smaller ones across front of cake, then deeper large garland below pillar. Continue around side. Pipe tube 18 zigzag garlands. Trim with tube 3 strings, tube 17 fleurs-de-lis and stars. Edge separator plate with tube 17.

ON MIDDLE TIER, pipe tube 20 bottom shell border and tube 18 top shell border. Drop guidelines from marks, then pipe tube 18 zigzag garlands. Add tube 3 strings, tube 17 fleurs-de-lis and rosettes.

ON TOP TIER, pipe a tube 18 shell border at base. Drop guidelines and pipe tube 18 zigzag garlands. Trim with tube 3 strings. Pipe top shell border with tube 18. Add tube 17 rosettes at points of garlands.

Add final trims

Secure ornament between pillars, then trim cake with petunias, securing them on mounds of icing and pushing spiked flowers into side of cake. Insert a flower spike into top of cake and arrange stemmed petunias in it. Surround with more flowers. Pipe tube 69 leaves. Two lower tiers of Ruffled Petunia serve 186, top tier, 30.

Serenade

Golden flowers and an intriguing Cherub separator set make this lovely cake unique and memorable.

ASSEMBLE ACCESSORIES: Angelic separator; bridge from Filigree stairway; Bridal couple figures.

Pipe royal icing flowers

Pipe two-tone roses with tubes 102 and 104, wild roses with tube 103 and tiny rosebuds with tube 102.

Prepare and decorate the tiers

BAKE, FILL AND ICE the two-layer round tiers 16" x 4", 12" x 4" and 8" x 4". Bake a single-layer 6" round tier for top.

Assemble on a 20" cake board with separator. Divide two lowest tiers into sixteenths and mark midway on sides. Divide 8" tier into twelfths and mark near base. Press a 2" cookie cutter on side of tier to mark four evenly spaced circles.

DECORATE TWO LOWER TIERS as a unit. On base tier, pipe a tube 4B bottom shell border. Pipe a "feathered" colonial scroll on side of tier, using marks as guide, with tube 15. On top of tier pipe scallops with tube 16, then add a tube 22 top shell border.

On 12" tier, pipe a tube 22 base shell border. Drop parallel tube 15 strings on side of tier, add tube 17 fleurs-de-lis. Edge plate with tube 15.

DECORATE TWO UPPER TIERS as a unit—8" tier on upper separator plate. Outline circles with tube 14. Pipe tube 18 shell borders at top of 8" tier, bottom and top of 6" tier.

TRIM WITH FLOWERS. Pipe tube 2 curving stems on side of 6" tier and attach rosebuds. Attach flowers to bridge with royal icing. Trim vase on separator with rosebuds and wild roses, then form six lavish sprays of flowers on 12" tier. Pipe tube 65 leaves.

Put it all together . . .

on the reception table. Pipe tube 14 curves of string from mark to mark at base of 8" tier. Drop hanging string and stars below. Set bridge and couple on cake top. Serenade is radiant! Serve two lower tiers to 186 guests.

Butterfly

An airy little butterfly flutters above a bouquet of silk flowers. More flowers fill miniature baskets. This impressive cake is very quick to decorate.

ASSEMBLE ACCESSORIES: 18″, 14″ and 10″ plates (from Tall tier stand); 7¾″ and 6½″ columns; Heart bowl; eight Flower baskets; silk flowers.

Prepare trims in advance
Pipe butterfly on net, using patterns and directions in Appendix. Arrange flowers in bowl as described on page 38. Add butterfly. Ice little blocks of styrofoam in baskets and arrange flowers.

Bake and decorate tiers
Bake, fill and ice the two-layer tiers—16″ x 4″, 12″ x 4″, and 8″ x 3″. Assemble on plates with columns.

Divide 16″ tier into 20ths and mark on side about 1½″ up from base. Divide 12″ tier into tenths and mark near base. Divide top tier into 16ths and mark on side 1″ up from base.

ON BASE TIER, pipe a tube 18 bottom shell border. Drop tube 16 string over it from mark to mark. Pipe eight-petal flowers with tube 16. Add tube 14 star centers. From top edge, drop tube 16 string. Finish with tube 17 upright shells and stars. On top of tier pipe tube 14 scallops and stars, then a tube 17 top shell border.

ON BOTTOM OF 12″ TIER, pipe a tube 18 upright curved shell at mark, then fill in with shells to next mark. Continue around cake. Pipe a "feathered" colonial scroll with same tube, using upright shells as guides. Pipe tube 14 scallops on top of tier, then a tube 17 top shell border.

ON TOP TIER, pipe a tube 17 base shell border, then drop tube 14 string. Top with tube 17 fleurs-de-lis. Drop tube 14 string from top edge, then pipe a tube 17 top shell border. Pipe scallops on top with tube 14.

Set bouquet on top of cake and flower baskets on base tier. Two lower tiers of Butterfly will serve 186 guests.

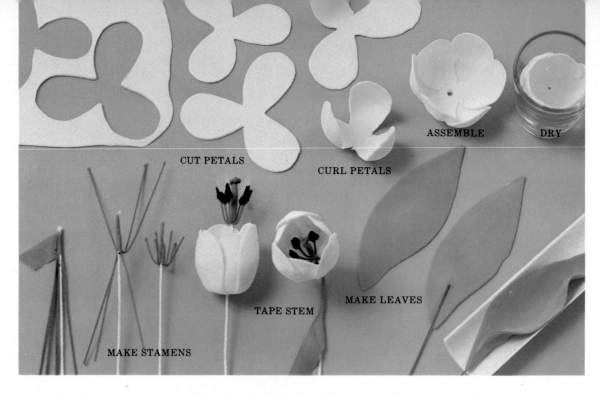

CUT PETALS CURL PETALS ASSEMBLE DRY

MAKE STAMENS TAPE STEM MAKE LEAVES

Tulip

A classic, pure white cake sets off two lovely arrangements of golden gum paste tulips. You'll enjoy fashioning the flowers with a fast, easy technique—and the little vases may be treasured for years to keep wedding memories glowing.

ASSEMBLE YOUR ACCESSORIES
Flower garden cutter set
Two Heart bowl vases
14 Filigree bells, 2" size
Four 10" Roman pillars
Two 14" separator plates
Eight Angel musicians
Eight Small doves

Make the tulips in advance

If you've never worked with gum paste before—start here! Tulips are the quickest and easiest to make of all gum paste flowers.

FORM FLOWERS. Form the flowers one day, then assemble them the next. You'll need about a dozen. Make a recipe of gum paste (Chapter 9). Take out about a fifth of the batch and tint. Work with one flower at a time. Roll out a small portion about $1/16"$ thick. Cut out one petal section with the small tulip cutter and one with the large tulip cutter. Lay the two sections on a piece of foam toweling and curl each petal by pressing with your thumb from the edge of the petal to the center. Brush the center of the large section with egg white, then press the small section to it. Make a hole in the center with pointed end of a stick. Dust the inside of a shot glass with corn starch and place

flower within it. Continue for more flowers. Dry overnight.

ASSEMBLE TULIPS. Make centers for all flowers. Tape a long piece of stiff florists' wire and six short pieces of fine florists' wire together. Bend the fine wires up to surround the taped portion. Clip off all wires to about ¾". Coat the taped section by inserting it into a decorating cone fitted with tube 10 and filled with green royal icing. Squeeze lightly as you pull out wire. Pipe three tube 3 dots on end.

Insert tips of fine wire into a decorating cone filled with black icing and fitted with tube 6. Squeeze lightly and pull out to form stamens. Dry all centers. Insert the wire into hole in the tulip, then wrap exposed stem with floral tape.

ARRANGE TULIPS. Cut a 3" styrofoam ball in half and secure halves in bowls with royal icing. Cover exposed styrofoam with green royal icing, then insert tulip stems, clipping as necessary. Fill in with gum paste leaves, or pipe them with tube 112.

Bake and decorate tiers

You will need three two-layer round tiers—16", 12" and 8". Two larger tiers should have a height of 4"—top tier is 3" high. Fill, ice and assemble on cake board with plates and pillars. Divide base tier into 14ths and mark at top edge. Divide center tier into eighths and mark near top. Lightly press a pattern press at each division.

DECORATE BASE TIER. Pipe reverse shell bottom border with tube 32. Drop string guidelines for garlands from mark to mark, leaving ½" open space between each. Pipe tube 17 zigzag garlands, then drop triple strings with tube 4. Pipe zigzag tube 14 scallops on top of cake, matching them with side garlands. Use tube 17 for reverse shell top border. Edge separator plate with tube 14 curves, then drop tube 4 string over them.

DO TWO TOP TIERS as a unit. On 12" tier, outline marked patterns with tube 14 reverse shells. Pipe tube 22 star base border, then drape with tube 4 string. Pipe a tube 17 shell border at top.

On top tier, pipe a tube 3 wavy line all around the side. Pipe curved branches extending up and down, then add lily of the valley blossoms with tube 81, and long slender leaves with tube 66. Pipe a tube 16 reverse shell bottom border. Use the same tube to pipe puffy garlands at top edge. Drape garlands with tube 4 string. Finish with "e" motion scallops on top of tier with tube 4.

Add finishing touches

Attach little doves to top tier with icing. Pipe mounds of icing on side of 12" tier and press in angels. Attach bells between garlands on base tier. Set tulips in place.
Two lower tiers of Tulip serve 186.

48

Posy

Even a cake of moderate size can look spectacular when adorned with a filigree stairway! Posy is an easy cake to decorate, but careful attention to all the pretty details make it a polished masterpiece. Notice the flower and ribbon trim on serving stands and pillars, ornaments and stairways.

ASSEMBLE ACCESSORIES
  Three Lazy daisy servers
  One 16" and two 14" plates (from Tall tier stand)
  Four 5" Grecian pillars
  Two 9" round separator plates
  Top plates from small and regular Heart bases
  Arch canopy trellis
  4" Filigree heart
  Three Small doves
  Bridal couple
  Bridesmaid and Groomsmen figures

Make trims in advance
PIPE DROP FLOWERS, in royal icing using tube 131 for larger blooms and tubes 224 and 225 for smaller ones. Set aside to dry.

FOR TOP ORNAMENT, glue arch to larger heart base. Glue ribbon bows and a dove at top of arch, then attach flowers with royal icing.

FOR SMALL ORNAMENT within pillars, glue heart to small base, then glue two doves in front of it. Add flower trim.

REMOVE PLATES from serving stands. Replace one with 16" plate and two others with 14" plates.

Prepare the tiers
FOR MAIN CAKE, base is a two-layer round, 14" x 4". Top tier is a two-layer 8" round, 3" high.

SATELLITE CAKES are two-layer rounds, 12" x 4" high.

Fill, ice and assemble all tiers on serving stands, adding plates and pillars to main cake. Divide each of the satellite cakes into sixteenths, marking about 1" above base. Divide bottom tier of main cake into twentieths, marking 1" above base. Divide top tier into twelfths and mark 1" below top of tier.

Decorate identical satellites
ON EACH CAKE, pipe a tube 18 shell border at base. Top this with deeply curved tube 22 scallops, piped from mark to mark. Pipe a curved shell, bringing it down to base of cake.

Pipe a second curved shell in opposite direction, meeting first shell at base.

Pipe similar scallops on top edge, using tube 18. Position them between scallops on bottom of cake.

TRIM WITH FLOWERS. At bottom of cake, mass flowers in triangle shapes, attaching with dots of icing. Use larger flowers at bottom, tapering to smaller flowers at top. Finish with a few buds (shell shapes piped with tube 3).

At top edge, form a little cascade starting between each scallop. Pipe a mound of icing and press in flowers, adding a few more at edges. Finish with tube 3 shell-shaped buds.

Decorate main cake
ON BASE TIER, pipe a tube 18 bottom shell border. Then pipe deeply curved shells from mark to mark with tube 22. At top edge, pipe tube 18 scallops, the same as top scallops on satellite cakes. Edge separator plate with tube 13.

ON TOP TIER, pipe tube 18 shell borders at bottom and top. Now pipe scallops on side from mark to mark—two curved shells joined.

TRIM WITH FLOWERS. On top tier, attach a little cluster of flowers at tops of scallops, ending with tube 3 shell-shaped buds.

On top of bottom tier, attach curves of flowers between each scallop, starting with larger flowers and ending with small flowers and tube 3 shell-shaped buds.

At bottom of tier, form flower curves in opposite direction, ending with buds.

Put it all together
Center main cake on the reception table. Set satellite cakes on either side, leaving about 1" of space between cakes. Have a helper hold stairways above cakes as you adjust position. Set ornaments in position.

Add ribbon bows and flowers to bases of servers. Attach flowers to top and bottom of stairways with icing. Wire tiny ribbon bows to railings. Pose the bridesmaids, groomsmen and finally the bridal couple. Posy is simply beautiful! Serve to 228, omitting top tier.

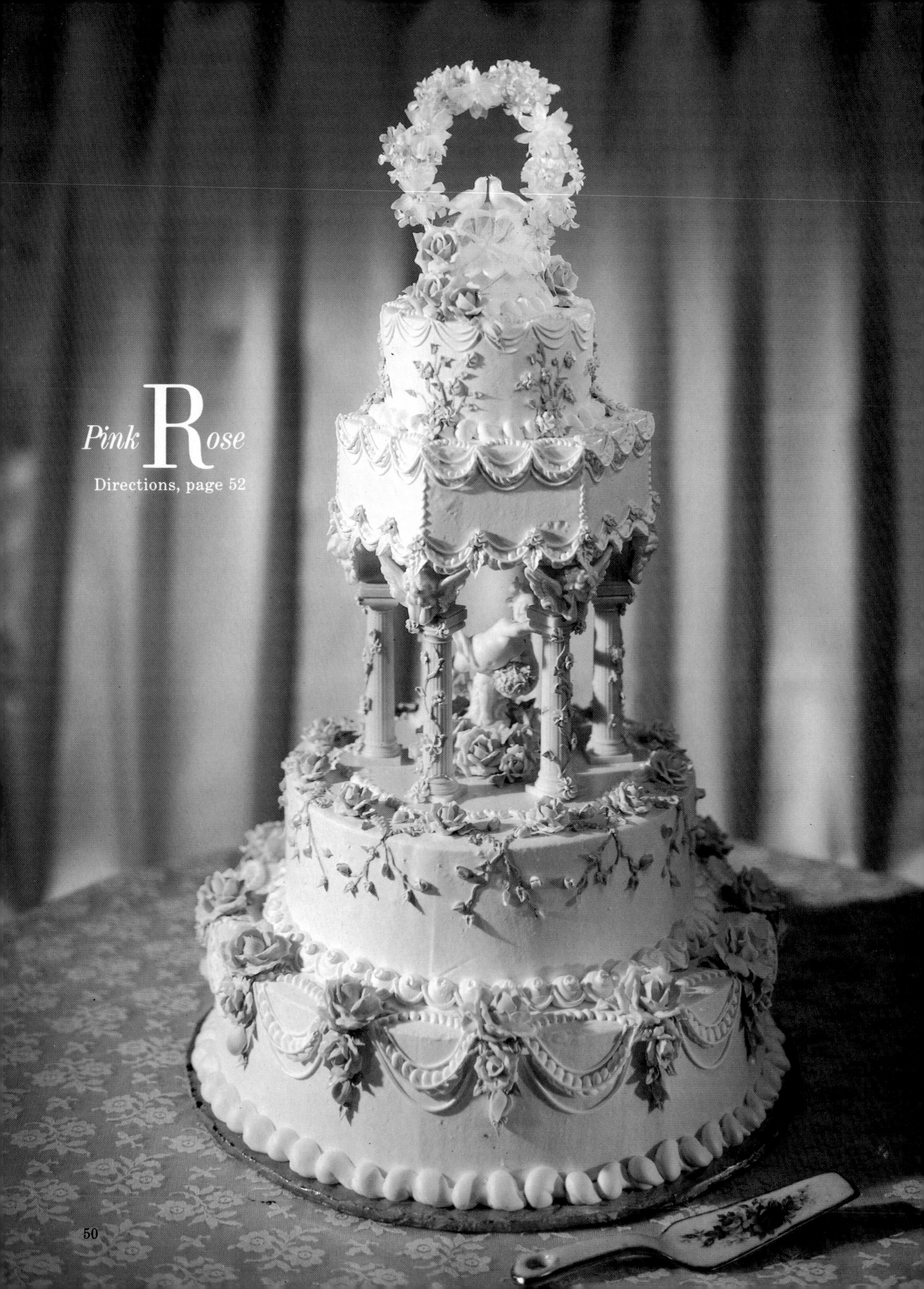

Pink Rose

Directions, page 52

White Rose
Directions, page 52

51

Pink Rose *page 50*

The rose, flower of romance, trims this dainty baroque cake. Note how even the pillars are decorated for a charming, harmonious effect.

ASSEMBLE ACCESSORIES: six 6½" Arched pillars; two 9" hexagon plates; six Angelinos; Frolicking cherub; top ornament.

Prepare flowers and trim

Pipe royal icing roses and buds with tubes 104 and 102, tiny rosebuds with tube 101, and drop flowers with tubes 504 and 506. Glue angelinos to tops of pillars.

Bake and ice tiers

You will need three two-layer round tiers—16", 12" and 6", each 4" high—and a two-layer 9" hexagon tier, 3" high. Bake, fill and ice, then assemble with plates and pillars. Divide base and top tiers into twelfths and mark at top edge.

Decorate the cake

DO TWO LOWER TIERS as a unit. On 16" tier pipe a tube 10 reverse shell border. Pipe circular-motion tube 6 garlands on side, leaving 1" space between each. Drop triple strings with tube 4 and use same tube for scallops on top of tier. On 12" tier pipe a tube 8 ball border at base and trim with tube 4 string. Pipe green zigzag scallops on top of tier with tube 4, then add curving branches on side. Attach tiny rosebuds. Edge plate with tube 4.

DO TWO UPPER TIERS as a unit. Start with top tier. Drop triple strings form top edge and pipe scallops on top with tube 4. Pipe tube 3 curving stems on side, then add tube 6 reverse shell border. On hexagon tier, pipe tube 5 bulbs down each corner. Pipe tube 5 garlands on side, scallops on top. Drape garlands with tube 4 string. Pipe base border at the reception table.

Add final touches

Attach ornament on top and trim with roses. Secure drop flowers on side of 6" tier. Set cherub within pillars and circle with roses. Arrange roses on lower tiers. Trim all flowers with tube 65 leaves.

ON THE RECEPTION TABLE, pipe base border on hexagon tier. Pipe circular-motion garlands with tube 5, allowing them to hang slightly below tier. Pipe a tube 72 leaf between each garland, then drape with tube 4 string and add drop flowers. Pipe a curving vine up each pillar and trim with drop flowers and tube 65 leaves. Three lower tiers of Pink Rose serve 208.

White Rose *page 51*

Unusual construction and lavish flower trim make this cake very impressive, very Victorian.

ASSEMBLE ACCESSORIES: four 7" Corinthian pillars; two 12" round plates, four large Cherub figures; top ornament.

Pipe royal icing flowers

Pipe tubes 125 and 104 roses, tube 104 sweet peas and tube 224 drop flowers. Following pattern, pipe four tube 17 hearts and dry on a curve. Ice a 4" styrofoam half-ball and cover with roses and sweet peas. Add tube 67 leaves.

Bake and ice two-layer tiers

Base tier is 14" x 4" square, middle tier 12" x 4" round and top tier 8" x 3" round. Assemble with pillars and plates. Divide top edges of base tier into fourths. Mark corresponding scallops on top of tier. (Use a cookie cutter.) Make a second series of marks 1½" up from base. Divide top edge of middle tier into twelfths, bottom edge into 24ths.

Decorate the cake

ON BASE TIER, pipe tube 16 "e" motion garlands at bottom. Drop strings from mark to mark for double garlands on sides of tier. Pipe lower garlands with tube 16, using an "e" motion and starting and ending with a curl. Pipe zigzag upper garlands with same tube. Pipe a tube 72 leaf between each. Fill in scallops with tube 3 lattice, then edge with zigzags of same tube. Edge plate with tube 14.

DO TWO UPPER tiers as a unit, starting at top. On top tier pipe a tube 19 shell border at top and drop tube 3 string. Pipe a tube 22 bottom shell border, trim with tube 13.

On 12" tier, drop string guidelines for double garlands on side. Do "e" motion top garland with tube 17, starting and ending with a curl. Pipe a tube 72 leaf between each. Cover string guidelines below with drop flowers. Do base border later.

TRIM CAKE with roses and cascades of sweet peas.

ON THE RECEPTION TABLE, assemble cake and pipe base border of 12" tier. Pipe zigzag garlands from mark to mark with tube 16, then pipe curves over them with same tube. Pipe ruffled tube 72 leaves. Attach piped hearts to pillars with royal icing, then cover with drop flowers. Serve two lower tiers of White Rose to 166 guests.

Tiers in unusual proportions, lavish borders and fluffy flower trim add up to an elegant little masterpiece.

ASSEMBLE ACCESSORIES: four 5" Grecian pillars; two 6" separator plates; four cupid figures; Angel fountain; top ornament. Cover an 18" cake board with foil. (This is extra-large to accomodate borders.)

Pipe flowers, prepare tiers

In royal icing, pipe tube 104 sweet peas and tube 131 drop flowers. Fill cherub fountain with sweet peas.

BAKE, FILL AND ICE two-layer tiers—12" x 4", 10" x 4" and 6" x 3". Assemble on cake board. Divide top edge of bottom tier into 16ths. About 1½" down from top, make a second series of marks. Divide top edge of 10" tier into twelfths. Divide top tier into twelfths and mark about ½" up from base.

Decorate the cake

DO TWO LOWER TIERS, as a unit, working from top down. On middle tier pipe a tube 14 reverse shell base border. Drop string guidelines and pipe garlands with tube 3, starting and ending with a curl. Drop tube 3 string below garlands, then add tube 72 ruffled leaves. Pipe tube 3 zigzag scallops on top of tier and around plate.

ON BOTTOM TIER, pipe tube 16 upper garlands from mark to mark. Trim with double tube 3 strings. From lower marks, pipe a second series of tube 16 garlands, top with tube 3 string, then pipe tube 72 leaves. Finish with tube 3 bows and string. For bottom border, pipe tube 18 garlands and frame with a tube 16 dropped string. Pipe a tube 72 ruffled leaf between every other garland. Pipe tube 16 reverse shell top border.

ON TOP TIER, pipe a tube 16 reverse shell top border. Do bottom border when cake is on the reception table. Finish with cascades and clusters of sweet peas, tube 65 leaves.

ON THE RECEPTION TABLE, do base border of top tier. Drop tube 14 string from mark to mark, then pipe "e" motion garlands over string. Cover with curves. Add tube 72 leaves. Attach drop flowers to pillars. Place cupids and top ornament. Two lower tiers of Yellow Sweet Pea serve 116 guests.

Yellow Sweet Pea

CREATING YOUR FIRST WEDDING CAKE? Here's a beauty that employs only basic techniques. Only one tube is used for borders and trim! If you're an experienced decorator, Rosy Future will be your choice when you're in a real hurry for a lovely cake.

ASSEMBLE ACCESSORIES: two 10″ round separator plates; four 5″ Corinthian pillars; petite top ornament; 18″ foil-covered cake board.

Pipe royal icing roses.

You can do this even weeks ahead with tube 104. You'll need about 32 roses and 16 buds. Pipe spikes on backs of five roses and three buds with tube 6.

Prepare the two-layer tiers

Base tier is 14″ round, middle tier 10″, top tier 6″. Bake layers so two lower tiers are 4″ high, top tier 3″ high. Fill and ice all tiers. Assemble with plates and pillars. Divide top tier into eighths and mark 1″ below top on side. Mark center front and back of middle tier, 1″ below top. Divide base tier into twentieths and mark midway on side.

Decorate the cake

ON BASE TIER, pipe colonial scroll on side, using marks as guides. Omit two scrolls at center front. Tube 16 is the only tube you'll need. Go back and "feather" the scrolls with curved shells, blending them into the main curves. Pipe shell borders at top and bottom of tier. Edge separator plate with scallops.

DO TWO UPPER TIERS as a unit. On top tier pipe fleurs-de-lis all around side, using marks as guides. Finish with stars. Pipe shell borders on both tiers. On middle tier, pipe a fleur-de-lis at center front and back, then add stars.

TRIM WITH ROSES. Set ornament on top and secure roses and a bud, tilting them on mounds of icing. Make a little spray of flowers on each side of middle tier, ending with a spiked rose and bud. Pipe a mound of icing on separator plate and arrange flowers. On cake board, secure a row of roses and buds, then use spiked flowers to form triangular shape on side of base tier. Trim all flowers with tube 68 leaves. Rosy Future is complete and lovely! Serve two lower tiers to 140 guests.

Rosy Future

*S*pring

Directions, page 56

Flower basket

A cake with a perky young personality! A little basket of silk flowers rests between the tiers. It will be treasured as a memento by the bride.

ASSEMBLE ACCESSORIES: three 7″ Corinthian pillars; two 9″ Heart separator plates; Floral scroll ornament base; Bridal couple figures; small wicker basket; two Flower spikes; silk flowers and ribbon.

Make trims in advance

Wedge a block of styrofoam into basket and arrange flowers, adding poufs of tulle and loops of ribbon. Make two little bouquets for base tier. Trim ornament base by twisting stems of several flowers together and inserting in openings of base. Tape stems on inside.

Prepare the two-layer tiers

Base tier is 16″ x 4″ round, then 12″ x 4″ and 9″ x 3″ heart tiers. Top tier is a single-layer 6″ x 2″ heart. Bake, fill and ice the tiers and assemble on 20″ cake board with pillars and plates.

Divide base tier into sixteenths and mark 1″ above bottom. Divide each side of 12″ heart tier into sixths and mark 1″ above bottom. Divide each side of 9″ heart tier into fifths and mark 1″ above bottom.

Decorate the cake

ON BASE TIER, pipe a tube 18 bottom shell border. Pipe tube 126 swags from mark to mark and add dots with tube 3. Just above swags, pipe parallel curves with tube 2B. Pipe hearts with tube 14. Finish with a tube 18 reverse shell top border.

ON 12″ HEART TIER, repeat the shell-swag-curve base border, the same as on base tier. Above it, add tube 14 strings and shells. Pipe a tube 17 top shell border. Edge separator plate with tube 14.

ON 9″ HEART TIER, pipe a tube 16 shell border at bottom and top. Over bottom border, pipe tube 125 swags and tube 14 hearts.

ON TOP TIER, cover sides with basket weaving. Pipe vertical lines with tube 5, horizontal strokes with tube 47. Add tube 15 bottom and top borders.

Put it all together

Insert flower spikes on either side of point of 12″ heart tier. Fill with small bouquets. Set basket within pillars, ornament base on top. Pose bridal couple. Flower basket is pretty as a picture! Serve three lower tiers to 194 guests.

Spring
shown on page 55

As fresh as an April morning! Pipe the regal lilies ahead of time—then decorating the cake is a joy.

ASSEMBLE ACCESSORIES: four 7″ Corinthian pillars; two 12″ round separator plates; Heart base; Bridal couple.

Pipe lilies in advance.

You will need about 65. Using tube 72, a 1⅝″ lily nail and royal icing, pull out three pointed petals. Then pipe three more, one between each. Center with a tube 13 star and set in artificial stamens. Pipe long slender leaves on wires with tube 65. Let flowers and leaves dry. Mount about half the lilies on wire stems. For between-tiers arrangement, ice a 3″ half-ball of styrofoam, edge with tube 14 shells. Insert stems of flowers and leaves into half-ball.

Prepare the two-layer tiers

Bake, fill and ice a 14″ x 4″ square base, a 10″ x 4″ round and a 6″ x 3″ round for the top. Assemble with plates and pillars on 18″ cake board.

Decorate the cake

ON BASE TIER, pipe a tube 22 reverse shell border at bottom and tube 17 shells at corners. Edge separator plate with tube 17 and a swirling motion. For top fleur-de-lis border, pipe three tube 17 shells on top of tier, then two curves below them on side. Finish with a tube 17 star. Repeat to complete border.

ON MIDDLE TIER, pipe a reverse shell tube 22 base border. Repeat fleur-de-lis top border the same as on 14″ tier.

ON TOP TIER, pipe four tube 17 fleur-de-lis on sides. Then add tube 17 reverse shell borders at bottom and top.

Add final trims

Set lily arrangement within pillars. Glue bridal couple to base, and place on top tier. Attach lilies and leaves with royal icing.

Arrange more lilies on top of 10″ tier and on sides of 14″ tier. Two lower tiers of Spring serve 146 guests.

*F*lower basket

Daisy Chain

As fresh as a summer morning!

ASSEMBLE ACCESSORIES: two 6″ hexagon plates; six 5″ Corinthian pillars; six Winged angels; Cardholding cupid, two Small doves; top plate from small Heart base; Flower spike.

Pipe royal icing daisies

Use tubes 102 and 103. Add tube 5 centers and dry within curves. You'll need about 125. Mount about 50 daisies on wire stems. Pipe tube 67 leaves on wire. Twist stems of leaves and flowers into bouquets— six small bouquets for base of cake and a larger one for within pillars. Tie with ribbons.

Pipe tube 5 spikes on backs of remaining flowers (for garlands). Glue cupid to plate, doves to hands.

Bake and ice the tiers

All are two-layers—a 15″ x 4″ hexagon, 10″ x 4″ round and 6″ x 3″ hexagon. Assemble with plates and pillars on cake board.

Mark curves on sides of all tiers. On round tier, divide in sixths, using tier below as guide, and mark midway on side. Within marks, divide in thirds, mark 1″ above base.

Decorate the cake

DO TWO LOWER TIERS as a unit. On round tier, pipe a tube 7 bulb border at base, a tube 5 bulb border at top. Drop tube 2 double strings from mark to mark on side. Edge separator plate with tube 16. On bottom tier, pipe a tube 7 bottom bulb border. Fill in curves with tube 1 cornelli lace, extending up to base of round tier. Edge curves and define corners with tube 3 beading.

ON TOP TIER, fill in areas from base to marked curves with tube 1 cornelli. Pipe a tube 5 bottom bulb border. Edge curves with beading piped with tube 2.

ADD TRIMS. Set ornament on top. Insert flower spike just behind it and arrange a few stemmed daisies and leaves. Attach winged angels to sides of top tier with icing. Set large bouquet within pillars. Using marked curves as guide, push in spiked daisies to form garlands. Trim with tube 67 leaves. Top with ribbon bows and daisies. Set small bouquets at base of cake. These are mementos for members of the wedding party. Serve two lower tiers of Daisy Chain to 114 guests.

ROMANTIC SYMBOLS of love decorate this prettiest of cakes.

ASSEMBLE ACCESSORIES: two 8″ separator plates; four 5″ Grecian pillars; two Small doves; Bridal couple; top plate from small Heart base.

Pipe royal icing trims

Use tubes 102 and 103 for roses, 102, 103 and 101s for wild roses and tube 106 for drop flowers. Mount flowers on wire stems and tie with ribbons for top bouquet. For flower garlands on middle tier, pipe tube 5 spikes on backs of roses and wild roses. Pipe twelve deep pink and twelve white hearts with tube 7 on wax paper. Pipe six double hearts in pale pink. Glue couple to plate.

Bake and ice tiers

All round tiers are two-layer—14″ x 4″, 10″ x 4″ and 6″ x 3″. Assemble with pillars and plates. Divide 6″ tier into sixths and mark midway on side. Divide 10″ tier into sixths and mark at top edge. Divide 14″ tier into twelfths and mark at bottom.

Decorate the cake

DO TWO LOWER TIERS as a unit. On 10″ tier, pipe puffy tube 17 garlands around bottom. Drop strings as guides for flower garlands, then pipe a tube 17 shell border at top. Edge separator plate with tube 16 zigzags.

On 14″ tier, pipe tube 199 upright shells at marks to form columns. Squeeze bag to let build up, then use even pressure to pull up to top edge of tier. Fill in border with tube 21 garlands. Edge with tube 16 zigzags. Drop double string guidelines from column tops and cover with tube 14 "e" motion drapes. Pipe a tube 21 shell border at top edge.

ON TOP TIER, pipe tube 16 garlands at base, tube 16 shells at top.

ADD FINAL TOUCHES. Attach hearts to top and bottom tiers. Attach doves on top tier, then drop strings and loops with tube 2 from their beaks. Set couple within pillars and trim with flowers. On middle tier, push in spiked flowers on string guidelines. Attach clusters of drop flowers at points. Trim with tube 65 leaves. Sweetheart is the prettiest cake a bride could dream of! Serve two lower tiers to 140 guests.

Sweetheart

Rose Garden

AS BEAUTIFUL as a garden!
This stately cake sets off an
arrangement of fresh roses with
lavish-looking side designs. Cooky
cutters mark patterns.

ASSEMBLE ACCESSORIES: eight 5″
Corinthian pillars; two 10″ and two
6″ round separator plates; Heart
cutter set; Card-holding cherub;
petite ornament; Heart base; fresh
flowers and florists' Oasis.

Bake the two-layer tiers
Square base tier is 14″ x 4″, middle
tier 10″ x 4″ round, top tier 6″ x 3″
round. Ice and assemble with plates
and pillars. On base tier, mark
center of each side. On middle tier,

divide in fourths and mark midway
on side. Do the same for top tier.

Now mark side designs with 2″ and
2½″ heart cutters. On base tier, use
2½″ cutter at center, then flank
with 2″ heart shapes. On middle
tier, mark four designs—2½″
hearts at marks with 2″ hearts
beside them. Mark four designs on
top tier with 2″ hearts.

PIPE DROP FLOWERS with tubes 33
and 225 and royal icing.

Decorate the cake
PIPE SIDE DESIGNS first with pastel
icing. Use tube 16 to outline
marked patterns with curved shells
and fleurs-de-lis. Add accents of

drop flowers and tube 65 leaves in
centers of designs.

PIPE SHELL BORDERS. On base tier,
use tube 22 for bottom border, tube
17 for top border. On middle tier,
use tube 17 at bottom, tube 16 at
top. On top tier, use tube 16 at
bottom, tube 15 at top.

ARRANGE FLOWERS. Turn heart base
upside down and line with clear
plastic wrap. Fill with oasis and
dampen, then arrange flowers. Set
within lower pillars. Place cupid
and ornament and Rose Garden is
complete! A beautiful cake, very
quickly decorated! Serve two lower
tiers to 146 guests.

Lily of the Valley

Directions, page 63

Maytime *at left*

As sweet and dainty as the bride!

ASSEMBLE ACCESSORIES: two 9" square separator plates; four 5" Corinthian pillars; four Mediterranean cupids; four Angelinos; petite ornament.

Pipe royal icing flowers

Do drop flowers with tube 129, wild roses with tube 101. Add tube 1 stamens and dry.

Bake two-layer tiers

You'll need a 16" x 4" round base tier, a 10" x 4" square and an 8" x 3" square. Fill, ice and assemble with plates and pilars on a ruffle-trimmed cake board.

Divide base tier into twelfths and mark side designs with a pattern press. Mark scallops on tier top with a cookie cutter corresponding to designs below. Divide each side of middle tier into fourths—mark at top edge. On top tier, press a pattern press in the center of each side.

Decorate the cake

DO TWO LOWER TIERS as a unit. On middle tier, edge separator plate with tube 14. Pipe a reverse shell base border with tube 15. Drop string guidelines for garlands from mark to mark, then pipe garlands with circular motions of tube 4. Drop double tube 2 string drapes, then add a row of parallel string drapes below. On top edge of tier, pipe a curving line with tube 3.

ON BASE TIER, fill in marked areas on side with loosely spaced tube 1 cornelli. Frame with tube 14, using "i" motion. Outline scallops on tier top with tube 15 reverse shells, and pipe reverse shell top border with same tube. Do zigzag bottom border with tube 87.

ON TOP TIER, pipe side designs with circular motions of tube 3. Do ruffled base border with tube 87.

Trim with flowers

Do top border of top tier. Pipe a thick line of icing, a few inches long, on top edge. Press in drop flowers. Continue to complete border. Add wild roses. Attach Angelinos on sides, then secure drop flowers in curves below them. Add flowers to top edge of middle tier and form little cascades on base tier. Finish with tube 65 leaves. Set cherub figures and ornament in place and serve two lower tiers of Maytime to 168.

Lily of the Valley

Shown on page 61

Curving sprays of lily of the valley circle the lower tiers of this refined pure white cake.

ASSEMBLE ACCESSORIES: six 5" Grecian pillars; two 10" hexagon separator plates; petite ornament; top ornament; six Angelinos.

Bake two-layer tiers

Base tier is 16" x 4" round, middle tier 12" x 4" round. Top tier is a 9" x 3" hexagon. Fill, ice and assemble.

Decorate the cake

DO TWO LOWER TIERS as a unit. Pipe a curving line around side of both tiers with tube 4 and add branches extending from curves. Pipe lilies of the valley with tube 79. This is one of the few flowers that may be piped directly on the cake. Touch the curved side of the tube to cake surface and press out a curve of icing. Continue pressure, moving tube in a slight circular fashion. Stop pressure and pull away. Result is a miniature bell. Add long slender leaves with tube 66.

ON MIDDLE TIER, edge separator plate with tube 14. For base border, pipe tube 22 upright shells, then drop a double row of tube 3 string over them. Pipe a tube 19 top shell border.

ON BASE TIER, do bottom border of tube 4B stars. Trim with tube 3 string. Pipe a tube 22 top shell border.

ON TOP TIER, use tube 17 to pipe a zigzag border at bottom, shell border at top. Attach an Angelino on each side with a mound of icing, then frame with curved tube 15 scrolls.

Set ornaments in position to complete the cake. Two lower tiers of Lily of the Valley serve 186 guests.

Daisy

Repeated curves and airy flower trim give this bridal cake a soft, feminine look.

Assemble accessories: two 10″ separator plates; four 5″ Corinthian pillars; four Mediterranean cupids; Kissing lovebirds ornament.

Prepare trim and tiers

Make royal icing daisies in varied sizes using tubes 125, 104 and 101. Pipe drop flowers with tube 131.

Bake, fill and ice two-layer tiers—16″ x 4″, 12″ x 4″, 10″ x 4″ and 6″ x 3″. Assemble with plates and pillars. Divide three lower tiers into twelfths and mark at top edges. On 10″ tier divide side of tier into 24ths and mark 1″ above bottom.

Decorate the cake

Do two bottom tiers as a unit. On 12″ tier, pipe a tube 32 puffy star border at base and drape with tube 3 string. Pipe "e" motion garlands with tube 17. Add a tube 352 ruffled leaf between each, then drape with tube 3 string. Outline curves on tier top with tube 3 and "e" motion. Finish with a tube 17 reverse shell top border.

On 16″ tier, pipe base border with tube 4B shells. Frame with tube 14 strings. Pipe "e" motion garlands with tube 17, add tube 352 leaves and drape with tube 4 triple strings. Do curves on tier top with tube 14 and "e" motion. Add tube 17 top shell border.

Do two upper tiers as a unit. Support separator plate on a 6″ styrofoam circle or pan, at least 2″ high, to allow for "hanging" border. On 6″ tier, pipe tube 19 stars at base, drape with tube 3 string. Pipe a tube 16 reverse shell top border.

On 10″ tier, pipe tube 14 garlands from mark to mark. Pipe a tube 349 leaf between each, then top with tube 4 string, starting and ending with a curl. Drop guidelines and pipe tube 6 "e" motion garlands from top edge, drape with tube 3 string. Pipe corresponding curves on tier top with tube 3 zigzags—then pipe a tube 14 reverse shell border at top edge.

Reassemble tiers with cupids and top ornament. Then trim Daisy with flowers, using smallest blooms at top, working down to largest. Serve three lower tiers to 234 guests.

Bridal bells
Directions, page 66

Bridal bells

Shown on page 65

A lavishly trimmed centerpiece, with all the elegance of the Edwardian era.

ASSEMBLE ACCESSORIES: two 8″ round separator plates; four 5″ Grecian pillars; four Snap-on filigree trims; four Mediterranean cupids; top ornament.

Do trims in advance

Pipe golden roses with tubes 104 and 127 in royal icing. When dry, pipe spikes on backs of 36 of the smaller roses. Pipe wild roses with tube 103. For between-tiers ornament, ice a small inverted paper cup with royal icing, then cover with smaller roses. Trim top ornament with wild roses.

Prepare two-layer tiers

Bake, fill and ice 16″ x 4″, 12″ x 4″ and 8″ x 3″ round tiers. Assemble with pillars and plates, first placing prepared ornament on separator plate. Divide two lower tiers in twelfths and mark at top edges. Divide top tier into sixteenths and mark at top edge and 1″ up from bottom.

Decorate the cake

DO TWO LOWER TIERS as a unit. On 12″ tier, pipe a puffy tube 4B shell border at base and trim with tube 4 string. Drop string guidelines from mark to mark on top edge of tier, then cover with tube 17 zigzag garlands. Add double tube 3 strings. Mark scallops on tier top and fill with tube 3 lattice. Edge with tube 3 bulbs. Finish top edge with tube 16 reverse shells.

ON BASE TIER, pipe a tube 4B star border at bottom, trim with tube 4 strings. Drop guidelines for garlands. Pipe a fluted curve with tube 102 and an up-and-down motion, then pipe tube 7 garlands. Trim with triple tube 4 string. Pipe tube 4 scallops on tier top, then do top reverse shell border with tube 17.

THE TOP TIER has a "hanging" bottom border, so attach separator plate to a 4″ circle of styrofoam, at least 2″ thick, to decorate. Drop string guidelines from mark to mark on side of tier, then pipe tube

14 garlands. Pipe a tube 3 zigzag curve above each garland, then drop a string over garland below. Pipe tube 16 puffy garlands at top edge of tier, drape with tube 3 string. Use same tube for zigzag scallops on tier top.

ADD CUPIDS and flower trim, forming cascades on base tier with spiked roses. Serve two lower tiers of Bridal Bells to 186 guests.

A LOVELY, FORMAL wedding cake wreathed with the bride's own flower. Orange Blossom is very easy to serve—lift off the flower clusters before cutting the cake.

ASSEMBLE ACCESSORIES: two 6″ round separator plates; four 5″ Corinthian pillars; Bridal couple figures; Heart base.

Pipe flowers in advance

Pipe royal icing orange blossoms on foil-covered number 4 or 5 flower nail. Pipe five tube 81 pointed petals, evenly spaced. Pipe two upright petals to form cup in center. Dry, then top cup with tube 1 dots. Mount on florists' wire stems. For buds, pipe a tube 5 ball on florists' wire. Add tube 1 sepals. Pipe tube 67 leaves on wires. Tape into clusters of three flowers, several buds and leaves. You will need twelve clusters for base tier, six for top tier and eight for between-tiers bouquet. To form, ice a 3″ half-ball of styrofoam and insert clusters.

Prepare two-layer tiers

You will need a 14″ x 4″ square tier and 10″ x 4″ and 6″ x 3″ round tiers. Fill, ice very smoothly and assemble on cake board with pillars and plates. Divide each side of 14″ tier into sixths and mark at base. Divide 10″ tier into sixths and mark on side near top. Mark heart designs with a 2″ cookie cutter. Divide 6″ tier into eighths and mark near base.

Decorate the cake

DO TWO LOWER TIERS as a unit. On 10″ tier, pipe a tube 18 bottom shell border. Pipe hearts with tube 16 and add stars. Edge separator plate with tube 16 scallops.

ON 14″ TIER, pipe tube 19 columns and tube 16 fleurs-de-lis. Complete base border with tube 16 stars. Drop tube 3 strings between columns. Add tube 16 stars.

ON 6″ TIER, pipe a tube 16 fleur-de-lis at each division. Pipe tube 16 base star border. Add tube 13 stars and a tube 16 top shell border.

COMPLETE THE TRIM. Attach bouquet to separator plate and reassemble tiers. Secure couple to base and set on top tier. Wreathe the ornament and 10″ tier with flower clusters. Two lower tiers of Orange Blossom serve 146 guests.

TIFFANY   AMERICAN HERITAGE   KORDES PERFECTA

CHRISTIAN DIOR

SIMONE

BEWITCHED

ROYAL HIGHNESS   DAINTY BESS

Rose ring

A glowingly beautiful, most unusual wedding cake! Rose Ring features the romantic rose in variety to create a centerpiece that's a lovely challenge to the decorator—a delight to the bride.

ASSEMBLE ACCESSORIES: four 7″ Corinthian pillars; Musical trio cherubs; 4″ circle of styrofoam, 1″ thick.

Pipe the flowers in advance

The flowers we used are all varieties of the beautiful hybrid teas, shown close up in the picture above. But you may choose your favorites, or the bride's, to copy in royal icing. Use tube 104 for each. After the flowers have dried, mount on florists' wire stems. Pipe tube 68 leaves on wire, then twist stems into clusters and bind with floral tape.

Make plate for ornament, using pattern and Color Flow technique, or cut plate from rolled gum paste. When dry, edge with tube 1 beading.

Ice styrofoam circle, dry, then attach pillars to circle with royal icing, bases touching.

Prepare the tiers

For the base, use a 14″ two-layer square. Upper tier is baked in a 10½″ ring pan. Ice and assemble on cake board.

On base tier, mark sides for scallop design. Midway on each side, make a mark 2½″ from each corner, then second marks 2½″ away. Sketch upper scallops with a toothpick above marks.

On ring tier, mark triangle design. Starting at center hole, and measuring carefully, mark 16 triangles, bases at center hole. Insert prepared circle, with pillars, into hole.

Decorate the cake

ON RING TIER, outline marked triangles with tube 2 beading. Add tube 8 ball borders.

ON BASE TIER, pipe a tube 8 ball border at bottom, trim with tube 5. Drop double tube 2 string from mark to mark, then pipe tops of scallops with tube 2 beading. Add graduated dots and stylized dot flowers with same tube. Edge top of tier with tube 8 balls, trim with tube 5.

Add flower trim

Push stems of roses into styrofoam circle to surround pillars. Attach Color Flow plate to tops of pillars with royal icing, then attach cherubs to plate. Arrange rose clusters in a wreath around ring tier. Beautiful Rose Ring is complete. Serve both tiers to 128 guests. If the bride would like a cake to freeze for the first anniversary, bake a second ring cake. At the anniversary celebration, she will adorn it with the unique ornament.

CHAPTER THREE

Lacy Latticed Wedding Cakes

THE MOST EXQUISITE bridal centerpieces are decorated with the most fragile trims—airy lattice, lace wings like delicate flying buttresses, dainty lace edging, even airborne top ornaments.

The small round tubes make all this magic possible. Using these simple tools and your own skilled hands, you can spin a thread of icing almost as fine as a hair.

LATTICE AND LACE WORK require an accurate, skillful hand to keep the icing lines true and even. You'll be more than repaid for your efforts when you see the lovely, finished masterpiece. We recommend you use *egg white royal icing* for most of this delicate work. You'll be surprised at the strength of the finished pieces when they're piped in this hard-drying icing. But just as a precaution—pipe more of the pieces than you plan to use. This allows for peace of mind in case of breakage. Use a small paper cone for best control when piping.

Lace Heart

Only plain round tubes are used for this dainty showpiece. They pipe the see-through heart at the top, the curved lace pieces, the fan-like trim on the base tier and the delicate heart-shaped box.

ASSEMBLE YOUR ACCESSORIES
Australian arch nails
Heart mini-cake pan
Four 7″ Corinthian pillars
Two 9″ separator plates

Pipe trims in advance

DO DROP FLOWERS in royal icing and tubes 224 and 225.

Mount about two dozen flowers on fine wire stems. Ice a 1″ half-ball of styrofoam and form bouquet by sticking stems into half-ball.

PIPE ALL LACE PIECES WITH TUBE 1 and egg white royal icing. For lace heart at top, tape pattern to stiff surface, tape wax paper over and pipe. When dry, turn over and pipe outline again for strength. Ice a 4″ length of stiff florists' wire, then attach to back of heart with a line of icing. About 2½″ of wire should extend from point of heart.

FOR CURVED LACE PIECES around 8″ tier, use the arch nail. Tape pattern to nail, tape wax paper over and rub with solid white shortening. Pipe pattern and dry. Place nail in warm oven for just a minute to melt shortening, then gently slide lace piece off. You will need eight.

FOR BETWEEN-TIERS BOX, use heart mini-cake pan as form. For lid of box, tape pattern to center of a heart shape, using pan upside down. Tape a piece of wax paper over pattern, then rub pan with solid white shortening. Pipe design, then fill in rest of area with lattice, making sure to stop lattice ¼″ from base of heart. Pipe a line of icing around edge. For lower part of box, rub heart shape on pan with shortening, then fill in entire area with lattice, again stopping ¼″ from base of heart. Place pan in warm oven for a minute, then release icing hearts.

Prepare the tiers

Base tier is a single-layer 16″ round, above it a 12″ x 4″ two-layer round. Next tier is a two-layer 8″ x 3″ round, at top, a single-layer 6″ round. Bake and fill the tiers, then ice with buttercream. Assemble on cake board with plates and pillars.

Divide base tier into sixteenths and mark ½″ below top edge. Divide 12″ tier into eighths and mark just below top edge. Transfer heart patterns to tier, following marks. Mark corresponding scallops on top of tier with a round cookie cutter. Divide 8″ tier into eighths and mark 1″ above base. Make a second series of marks midway between first to guide position of lace pieces.

Decorate the cake

FROM TINTED ROLLED FONDANT, cut fan shapes and crescents to surround 12″ tier. Gently press fan shapes to side of tier, using marked patterns above as guides. Press crescents to top of 16″ tier, meeting fans.

ON BASE TIER, pipe a tube 6 bottom ball border. Drop string guidelines from mark to mark, then pipe garlands with tube 6 and a back-and-forth movement. Top with tube 2 strings. Pipe a top ball border with tube 5.

ON 12″ TIER, fill in spaces between crescents with tube 4 balls. On top of tier, pipe tube 1 lattice, edge with tube 2 beading. Do top border with tube 4 beading. Pipe heart designs with tube 1, then over-pipe with same tube. Use tube 1 again to drop string from outer edge of fan to edge of crescent. Start at center point of fan and work to lower edge, then fill in other side. Edge with tube 1 beading, then tiny scallops.

ON 8″ TIER, do bottom border with tube 6 balls, then drop guidelines and pipe garlands with tube 6. Add tube 2 string and tiny hearts. Pipe top border with tube 4 balls. Do the same for borders of 6″ tier.

Add final trims

Push wire on heart into center of top tier. Trim tier with flowers. Attach curves of flowers to 8″ tier, using marks as guides. Now attach lace curves with dots of icing, holding each a minute until set.

With a hot nail or icepick, make a hole near center of separator plate on 12″ tier. Ice a 4″ length of stiff florists' wire and attach to back of heart box lid with icing, leaving about 2½″ of wire extending. When dry, push wire through hole in plate. Attach lower part of box to plate, then set bouquet within it on a small mound of icing. Form little cascades of flowers on bottom tier. Three lower tiers serve 156 guests.

Filigree Coronet

Lacy, lovely and daintily flowered! This impressive cake is truly easy to decorate. Just basic techniques are used, the drop flowers are quickly done and there's no need to pipe the filigree. Just press plastic filigree swirls in place! Stairways give a final dramatic touch.

ASSEMBLE YOUR ACCESSORIES

24 Filigree swirls
Frolicking cherub
Bride and groom figures
Bridesmaid figures
Five top plates
  from Petite heart base
Four Musical trio cherubs
Two 7" round separator plates
Four 7" Corinthian pillars
Complete Filigree stairway set

Prepare tiers and trim

PIPE DROP FLOWERS in royal icing and tubes 25, 30 and 35.

PREPARE TIERS. First make a 14" x 36" cake board of triple thickness of corrugated cardboard. Cover board with foil.

Base tier is a two-layer sheet cake, 18" x 12" x 4". Middle tier is a two-layer 10" x 4" round, top tier is 6" x 3". Assemble on cake board with pillars and plates.

Divide top tier into twelfths and mark midway on side. Divide middle tier into sixteenths and mark near top edge. On base tier, measure 2½" in from each corner and mark at base. On long sides of tier, make two additional marks at 2" intervals from first marks. These will guide piped columns.

Decorate the cake

ON FRONT OF BASE TIER, pull up columns with tube 32, making them shorter as you move in to center of tier. Pipe columns on short sides of tier and at back, then complete bottom border with tube 16 garlands. Connect columns at front and back with double tube 13 string. Pipe a tube 16 zigzag garland in center of tier, then over-pipe for full effect. Pipe zigzag garlands at corners of tier and press in flowers. Finish tops of columns with tube 16 fleurs-de-lis and stars. Use same tube for curved shell top border.

On MIDDLE TIER, pipe bottom border with tube 16 garlands. Drop double tube 13 strings from mark to mark, then pipe a large tube 16 garland at front and back of tier. Cover with drop flowers. Pipe a tube 16 reverse shell top border.

ON TOP TIER, pipe a tube 16 shell border at base, a tube 14 garland border at top. Drop double tube 2 string from mark to mark.

Complete the trim

Secure musical cherubs to top plates and attach flowers to plate with icing. Ring another plate with flowers, set within pillars and attach figures of couple. Set bridge on cake top, trim with flowers and secure cherub. Set stairways in position and trim with flowers. Attach filigree swirls to top and middle tiers. Pose the bridesmaids and the lovely picture is complete! Serve two lower tiers of Filigree Coronet to 156 guests.

Arabesque

Lattice and lacy wings trim the most ethereal wedding cake crowned by an airy little lattice temple. Arabesque is spectacular, but only basic techniques and careful planning are needed for its creation.

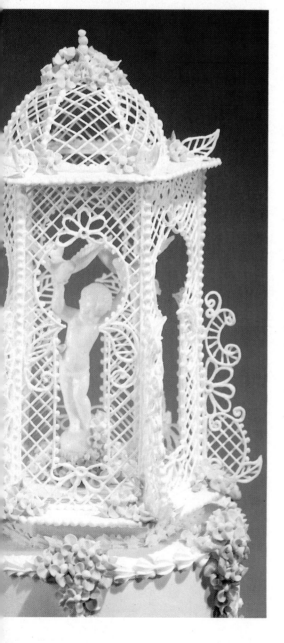

ASSEMBLE YOUR ACCESSORIES:
Two 12" separator plates
Four 7" Corinthian pillars
Bridal couple figures
Top plate from Heart base
Cherub card holder.

Pipe trims in advance

Pipe dainty drop flowers in royal icing with tubes 191, 224 and 225. Use varied tints of blue.

Using patterns, pipe twelve lace wings and the pieces for the top ornament with egg white royal icing and tube 1. For dome on ornament, grease a 3" ball half-mold with solid white shortening. Mark mold in six sections and fill each section with lattice, then pipe beading to define sections and finish edge. When thoroughly dry, place mold in a warm oven for a few minutes and gently push off dome. Tape all other patterns to a stiff surface, cover with wax paper, pipe the designs and dry flat.

Using patterns, cut lower and upper bases, side wall support and roof from rolled gum paste. Dry thoroughly.

Construct the ornament

Secure all pieces with royal icing. Stack lower base, upper base and wall support, centering each carefully. Glue small plastic doves to hands of card holding cherub and attach figure to center of wall support. Ring base with flowers. Pipe a line of icing against edge of wall support and set one wall section in position. Pipe icing against adjacent edge of wall support, and on one side of first wall section. Set second wall section in place. Continue until all wall sections are standing, then cover seams with beading. Dry, then pipe a line of icing on top of wall and set roof on it. Secure dome. Attach leaves to roof and lace wings at wall sides with dots of icing. Trim completed ornament with flowers.

Prepare the tiers

Base tier consists of two 16" round layers plus a 16" top bevel. Second tier is made up of two 12" layers, each layer 2" high. Third tier is an 8" round layer topped by an 8" top bevel. Top tier is a two-layer 6" round. Assemble on sturdy cake board with plates and pillars.

Divide and mark the tiers—16" tier into sixteenths, 12" and 8" tiers into twelfths, top tier into sixths.

Decorate the cake

ON 16" TIER pipe bottom shell border with tube 21, two borders that define bevel with tube 16. Drop string guidelines to define garlands and top of lattice at lower side of tier. Pipe zigzag garlands with tube 15, then pipe and over-pipe again to build up, pausing between pipings to let icing set. Do lattice, beaded edge and dropped string above with tube 2. Cover lower edge of lattice with tube 13 zigzags and add tube 14 fleurs-de-lis. On bevel surface, pipe tube 17 zigzag garlands, then trim with tube 2 string and tube 15 rosettes.

DO THREE UPPER TIERS as a unit. Wait until cake is assembled on the reception table to do base "hanging" border on 12" tier.

ON 12" TIER, pipe tube 17 shell border at top. Mark a circle with a 2" cookie cutter above spaces marked for every other garland and outline with tube 1 tiny scallops.

TRIM 8" AND 6" TIERS, with tube 16. Pipe shell borders, then zigzag garlands (garlands on 6" tier will be covered with flowers). Drop strings on 8" tier and pipe bows on 6" tier with tube 2.

Attach bridal couple to ornament plate and set within pillars. Now trim entire cake with flowers, covering garlands on 6" tier. Add leaves piped with tube 65.

Put it all together . . .

on the reception table. Pipe bottom border on 12" tier. Circle base with tube 17 shells, then pipe zigzag garlands from mark to mark with same tube. Add tube 2 string, tube 15 rosettes. Attach tiny clusters of flowers, add tube 65 leaves. Attach lace wings with dots of icing to 12" and 8" tiers. Crown the cake with the airborne ornament. Arabesque is exquisite! Serve three lower tiers to 216 guests.

White lace

This exquisite bridal cake is decorated with only the plain round tubes. Frilly lace sets off its sweet simplicity.

ASSEMBLE ACCESSORIES: two 8" round separator plates; four 5" Corinthian pillars; Cherub fountain; three Musical trio cherubs.

Pipe the flowers in advance

Pipe the dainty drop flowers in royal icing, using tubes 33, 224 and 225.

Pipe lace pieces

Tape patterns for lace pieces to stiff surface, tape wax paper smoothly over them. Pipe lace pieces with tube 1s and royal icing. You'll need 80 large and 72 smaller pieces.

Prepare the tiers

For bottom tier, bake a 16" base bevel layer, two 12" x 1½" round layers and a 12" top bevel layer. For top tier, bake an 8" x 2" round layer and an 8" top bevel layer.

BOTTOM TIER will be served as two tiers. First ice base bevel with buttercream and let crust. Cover slanted surface with rolled fondant. Assemble and fill 12" round layers and 12" top bevel as diagram shows—first a 12" layer, then a 12" cake circle covered with plastic wrap, then second 12" round layer and top bevel. Ice with buttercream, let crust, then cover with rolled fondant. Set on prepared base bevel layer.

FOR TOP TIER, fill and ice 8" round layer and 8" top bevel layer. Cover with rolled fondant. Assemble the two tiers with plates and pillars on a 20" cake board.

MARK TIERS. First tint a little fondant pale blue, roll out to ⅛" thickness and cut out a 3½" circle. Lay this on top of top tier. On top tier, divide at bevel into eighths. Mark scroll patterns at lower side of tier, centering below marks above.

On bottom tier, mark heart patterns, using pillars as guides. Transfer scroll pattern between hearts.

Decorate the cake

ON BOTTOM TIER, pipe a tube 7 ball border around outer edge of base bevel, then a tube 6 ball border at inner edge of bevel. Outline hearts with tube 2 beading, then use same tube to pipe inner scallops. Edge top bevel with tube 4 beading. Edge separator plate with tube 5 balls.

The scroll design is over-piped.

First pipe with tube 5, then with tubes 4, 3 and 2. Dry, then brush with thinned icing. Pipe tube 2 dots on base bevel surface and within heart designs.

ON TOP TIER, drop string guidelines from mark to mark to define curves. Pipe curves with tube 2 beading. Edge top of tier and blue circle with tube 4 beading. Pipe scrolls just as you did for bottom tier—first with tube 5, then with tubes 4, 3 and 2. Add tube 2 dots above curves.

Add dainty trims

Secure trio of cherubs on top of cake. Attach flowers in little clusters with dots of icing. Trim cherub fountain with flowers, then secure within pillars. Trim all flowers with tube 65s leaves.

Attach lace pieces, starting with top tier. Pipe a tiny tube 1 line of icing just below beading. Hold lace piece to it for an instant, just until set. Be sure to keep all lace pieces at a uniform angle. Attach lace pieces around hearts on lower tier the same way.

TO CARRY the cake to the reception site, remove top tier, with pillars, and attach to a second 8" separator plate. This will prevent bottom trim from being broken. Reassemble tiers on the reception table. White Lace is complete in its delicate beauty. Serve lower tier (as two tiers) to 136 guests.

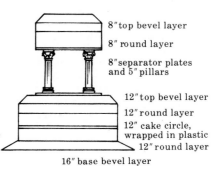

8" top bevel layer
8" round layer
8" separator plates and 5" pillars
12" top bevel layer
12" round layer
12" cake circle, wrapped in plastic
12" round layer
16" base bevel layer

Paradise

Very Victorian with its tasseled tiers, little gazebo and ornate bird cage ornament! Paradise is lavished with arrangements of fresh-looking green ferns, a most unusual and graceful trim.

ASSEMBLE YOUR ACCESSORIES
Two 13" Hexagon separator plates
Two 9" Hexagon separator plates
Twelve 7" Corinthian pillars
Eight 2" Filigree bells
Lower part of Petite heart base
Two Flower spikes
Small dove
1" Filigree bell

Pipe all trims in advance

PIPE OVAL SIDE PIECES for base tier in royal icing. Note that each oval design is done in two pieces. Tape pattern to an 18" curved surface, tape wax paper smoothly over it and pipe design with royal icing and tube 3. Over-pipe all lines with tube 2 for a dimensional effect.

PIPE LATTICE FENCE pieces. Tape pattern to stiff surface, tape wax paper over it and pipe with tube 2. When dry, turn over and pipe all edges again for strength. Pipe scrolls for fence and for bird cage on wax paper.

PIPE BIRD CAGE pieces. Tape patterns for side panels and door to stiff surface, tape wax paper over them and pipe with tube 2 and royal icing. Over-pipe all main lines for strength. Tape roof patterns to 8" curved surface, tape wax paper over and pipe with tube 2. Over-pipe edges. Add trim to ornament base by filling in circular areas with tube 2 lattice.

For bird cage base, roll out gum paste 1/8" thick, then cut, following pattern. Do the same for collar that supports roof.

For blue bird, paint a small plastic dove with thinned royal icing. "Glue" to top of 1" bell with icing.

Make banner by gluing a 1½" long triangle of blue paper to a 2" length of cloth-covered florists' wire. Pipe tube 2 tiny heart.

ASSEMBLE BIRD CAGE. Use royal icing as glue. On center front panel, pipe a line of icing on left side of opening. Set oval door on it in open position. Prop until dry. Attach gum paste base to prepared ornament base. Secure blue bird to center of base. Pipe a line of icing on bottom of center back side panel and set on base. Pipe icing on bottom and side of adjoining panel and join to first panel. Continue adding panels, propping each for a few minutes until set. Add center front panel last.

Pipe a line of icing on top of completed wall and set collar on it. Add roof sections. Pipe a line of icing on bottom of center back section and set on collar. Do the same for center front section. Hold until set. Continue adding sections directly opposite each other. Pipe a ball of icing at top of roof and insert flag. Attach scrolls with dots of icing and cover all seams with tube 2 bulbs.

MAKE FERN ARRANGEMENTS. Cut fine florist wire in 4" lengths. Push each wire into bag of green icing fitted with tube 3. Pull out wire, curving as you go, and lay on wax paper to dry. On each wire, pipe long, jiggly tube 65s leaves, tapering as you approach top. Prepare eight vases for ferns. Pipe a large tube 32 rosette on wax paper, set a 2" bell upside down on it. Dry. Line bells with clear plastic, fill with white royal icing and insert ferns.

Prepare the tiers

Bake, fill and ice two-layer tiers, 18" x 4" round, 12" x 4" hexagon and 8" x 3" round. Assemble on cake board or tray with plates and pillars. Divide 18" tier in sixths and mark at top edge. Divide 8" tier into sixths and mark midway on side.

Decorate the cake

ON BASE TIER, pipe shell border at bottom with tube 32. Pipe top rope border with tube 20. Edge separator plate with tube 17. From marks on top edge of tier, drop two tube 17 "ropes" for tassels. Pipe tassels with tube 4, building up for full effect. Attach oval side pieces, joining at centers, with dots of icing. Edge with tube 2 beading.

ON MIDDLE TIER, pipe base shells with tube 19. Do tube 2 string scallops above. Pipe tube 18 rope border at top of tier. Drop string guidelines for curves on side of tier, then pipe tube 16 rope. Pipe two tube 18 upright shells near base of tier up to rope curve. Pipe tube 2 lines to form tassels over them. Edge separator plate with tube 16.

ON TOP TIER, pipe base shell border with tube 18. Do rope border at top with tube 17. Drape six tube 16 garlands from mark to mark, add tube 2 string. Finish with a tube 18 upright shell at each point of separator plate. Add tube 18 star.

Put it all together . . .

on the reception table. Set a vase of ferns within pillars on hexagon tier. Pipe line of icing on bottom of one fence section and place on separator plate. Add second section, piping tube 2 dots at joint. Continue to complete fence. Edge base with tube 3 beading. Set vases of ferns on base tier. Set bird cage ornament on top tier. Insert flower spikes on either side of bird cage. Form two clusters of ferns, twisting stems together and wrapping with floral tape. Insert in spikes. A masterpiece! Paradise will serve 198 guests from two lower tiers.

Classique

Pure white, pure elegance. A dignified cake for a formal reception, Classique proves how simple borders, executed to perfection, can achieve a timeless beauty. Lattice and graceful string drapes enhance the tiers.

ASSEMBLE ACCESSORIES: two 10″ round separator plates; four 5″ Grecian pillars; two ornaments (for between-tiers and top).

Prepare two-layer tiers

Bake, fill and ice 16″ x 4″, 12″ x 4″ and 8″ x 3″ tiers. Divide base tier into 18ths and mark at top edge. Divide top tier into 12ths and mark at top edge.

Decorate the cake

DO TWO LOWER TIERS as a unit. On middle tier, pipe a shell border at base with tube 17 and trim each shell with a tube 102 ruffle. Pipe upright shells around top edge with tube 18, using about 1″ space for each shell. Trim tops of shells with tube 14 zigzags. Edge separator plate with same tube. *Do all stringwork on cake with tube 3.* From tail of each shell, drop short string drapes. Now drop longer double drapes from one shell to second shell over, in interlaced effect.

ON BASE TIER, pipe a star border with tube 22, trim with string. Drop string guidelines from mark to mark on top edge. Pipe garlands with tube 16 zigzags, then fill with lattice. Trim with string. Pipe scallops on tier top with tube 14 zigzags, then finish with tube 16 reverse shell top border.

ON 8″ TIER, pipe a tube 22 star border at base and trim with string. Drop guidelines from mark to mark on top edge, then pipe tube 14 "e" motion garlands. Drape with triple string. Pipe scallops on tier top with tube 14 and "e" motion. Pipe top shell border with same tube. Place ornaments on cake and Classique is perfection! Serve two lower tiers to 186 guests.

Moonbeam

Elegant and pristine, the lofty tiers of Moonbeam are separated by transparent pillars and draped with gossamer stringwork. This type of "hanging" string looks almost miraculous, but it's really not difficult.

ASSEMBLE ACCESSORIES: two 7″, two 9″ and two 13″ Clear plates; four 3″ and eight 5″ Clear pillars; Bridal couple; Silk flowers; four iridescent doves.

Prepare two-layer tiers

Base tier is 16″ x 4″, then a 12″ x 4″ and an 8″ x 4″ tier. Top tier is 6″ x 3″. Bake, fill and ice. Assemble with plates and pillars. Careful measuring is essential for the beauty of Moonbeam. Divide base tier into twentieths and mark at top edge and 1½″ above bottom. Divide 12″ tier into eighteenths and mark at top edge. Divide 8″ tier into twelfths and mark at top edge and 1½″ up from bottom. Divide 6″ tier into twelfths and mark at top and bottom edge.

Decorate the cake

ON BASE TIER, pipe tube 199 upright shells around bottom, positioning two shells between each mark. Bring shells up to level of marks. *Use tube 3 for all stringwork on cake.* Pipe double strings from tail of one shell, skip a shell and attach to tail of third. Continue around tier for interlaced effect. Add tube 16 stars at points. Drop strings from mark to mark on top edge of cake, then add a second row of string drapes and loops. Pipe tube 19 garlands around top edge of tier corresponding to string drapes. Edge separator plate with tube 16.

ON 12″ TIER, pipe puffy zigzag garlands from mark to mark at base with tube 18. Top with double strings and tube 16 stars. At top edge, drape with triple string in interlaced fashion, then do top shell border with tube 18. Edge separator plate with tube 16 shells.

ON 8″ TIER, pipe a tube 18 bottom shell border. Drape with string

Please turn the page

Ireland

A wedding cake spectacular! Ireland is enriched with "lattice" lace and touched with the fresh green of piped shamrocks. Create it to pay special tribute to a bride of Irish descent—or substitute the bride's choice of flowers for the shamrocks.

ASSEMBLE ACCESSORIES: two Small doves; four 5″ Grecian pillars; two 6″ separator plates; Kneeling cherub fountain.

Pipe shamrocks, prepare tiers

Use royal icing, tubes 102 and 103 and a number 7 nail for the shamrocks. Hold tube at a 45° angle, wide end down, touching center of nail. Turn nail and move out to its edge—move back to center, out to edge and back to center again for heart-shaped petal. Repeat for two more petals, add tube 2 stem.

BAKE, FILL AND ICE tiers to sizes as shown on diagram. Use a creamy "belleek"-colored buttercream (substitute butter for shortening).

Paint all accessories with thinned royal icing, tinted to match buttercream. Construct cake with pillars and plates.

Measure and mark tiers

Careful, accurate measuring gives Ireland its special charm, and makes decorating easy. On blossom cake at top, mark at each indentation, 1″ up from base.

ON 5″ TIER, divide in sixths and mark ¾″ down from top edge.

ON 10″ TIER, divide and mark top edge of bevel into twelfths. Do the same for lower edge of bevel, lining up exactly with marks at top of bevel. Now, divide and mark each of these spaces into thirds.

ON 12″ TIER, mark the same as on 10″ tier. Divide top edge and lower edge of bevel into twelfths, then divide each space into thirds. Repeat markings at base of 12″ tier.

ON BASE BEVEL TIER, divide outer edge into twelfths, then each space into thirds. Line up with marks above. Mark side curves on all tiers.

Decorate the cake

DO LOWER TIERS below pillars as a unit, starting at top. Edge separator plate with tube 6 balls.

On 10″ tier, do lattice with tube 2. Pipe radiating lines from separator plate to marks on upper edge of bevel, then diagonal lines to marks at lower edge of bevel. Cross with lines in opposite direction. Pipe five-dot flowers at intersections. Pipe marked curves with tube 2, adding dot flowers as shown.

On 12″ tier, pipe lattice and curves exactly as you did for 10″ tier, but use tube 3. Pipe a ball border at base of 10″ tier with tube 6.

On base bevel tier, pipe lattice and curves just as you did for two upper tiers, using tube 4. Add a tube 6 ball border at base of 12″ tier. Use same tube for bulb border at outer edge of base bevel.

DECORATE TOP TIER. Pipe a tube 6 ball border at bottom of 5″ tier. Do curves and top border with tube 2. Edge bottom of blossom cake with tube 2 and pipe curves with same tube.

Add finishing touches

Attach doves to top of cake and cherub within pillars. Now attach shamrocks with dots of icing in cascades and clusters. Ireland is spectacular! Cut base bevel separately into 34 servings, 12″ and 10″ tiers into 116 servings for a total of 150.

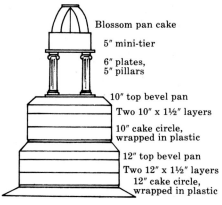

Blossom pan cake

5″ mini-tier

6″ plates, 5″ pillars

10″ top bevel pan
Two 10″ x 1½″ layers
10″ cake circle, wrapped in plastic

12″ top bevel pan
Two 12″ x 1½″ layers
12″ cake circle, wrapped in plastic

16″ base bevel tier

Insert dowels for support into base bevel, 12″ and 10″ tiers

Moonbeam *continued*

from mark to mark, then add tube 16 stars. Drop double strings from mark to mark at top edge, then add a third row of string drapes beneath them. Add tube 2 dot flowers. Finish top edge with tube 16 shells, edge plate with tube 14.

ON TOP TIER, pipe a tube 16 reverse shell base border. Drop double strings on top edge, then pipe a tube 16 top shell border.

Arrange clusters of flowers and secure to plates. Attach doves between pillars below top tier.

Finish the cake . . .

on the reception table. Now add all the tube 3 "hanging" string and loops. Start with the top tier and work down. The technique is the same as piping string drapes on the side of a tier.

Circle the tier, touching tube to edge of separator to attach, pulling straight out, then attaching again to separator plate. Let first row of string dry for just a few minutes, then pipe second row by touching tube lightly to center of string drape, then attaching to center of next drape. Add decorative loops.

Below 8″ and 12″ tiers add additional rows of string drapes, but keep areas between pillars free. Set bridal couple on top of cake—Moonbeam is enchanting! Serve three lower tiers to 216.

Ireland

R*ose* L*ace*

Shining poured fondant sets off the handsome "appliqued" lace designs on the tiers of Rose Lace. Use the patterns in the Appendix, or make your own pattern to repeat the lace on the bridal gown. The rich simplicity of the cake is enhanced by a glorious cascade of golden jubilee roses.

Cover a cake for the groom with chocolate fondant and trim it with the same golden roses.

ASSEMBLE ACCESSORIES: Kissing lovebirds ornament; Stairsteps.

Pipe roses in advance

Jubilee roses are very similar to a regular rose, but the tone-on-tone tints and furled petals make them outstanding. Use a number 13 flower nail, tube 126 and royal icing. Follow the steps in the picture. When you have completed piping the rose, dip your fingertips into cornstarch and pinch each yellow petal into a furled shape. Pipe smaller roses with tube 104. Pipe tube 67 leaves directly on wire. When dry, twist stems together into groups of three and bind with floral tape.

Prepare the tiers

All round tiers are two-layer—14″ x 4″, 10″ x 4″ and 6″ x 3″. Bake and fill the tiers, then ice smoothly with buttercream. When icing has crusted, cover with poured fondant. Set tier on a cake rack placed over a cookie sheet. Starting at center top of tier, pour the fondant with a circular motion, allowing it to flow down the sides. Have a spatula handy to touch up any bare spots. Let fondant harden, then assemble

Pipe double spiral and three petals in gold icing

Add five yellow petals

Furl petals

the tiers with dowels on an 18″ cake board.

Decorate the cake

TRANSFER LACE DESIGNS to tiers. Evenly space four designs on base tier, four on middle tier and two on top tier. We did the lace in pale ecru to contrast with the gleaming white fondant. Working from top tier down, outline the design with tube 1 and Color Flow icing straight from the batch. (Recipe is on Color Flow package.)

Now thin the icing to the consistency of thick honey. Fill a parchment cone, cut a tiny opening in the tip and flow in the design. Pipe tube 5 bulb borders in buttercream at bases of all tiers.

INSERT STAIRS. These make a convenient base for the rose cascade that you can easily remove at serving time. Starting at center front of base tier, push in pegs of stairs curving to center tier and ending at back of top tier. Secure lovebird ornament to top of cake. Secure roses to stairs on mounds of

icing, attaching two or three roses on top of cake. Add leaves. Two lower tiers of this masterpiece cake serve 140 guests.

The Groom's cake

This handsome, deep chocolate confection is trimmed with the same jubilee roses as the bridal cake. You will need about 15 flowers. Pipe royal icing spikes on the backs of three or four roses to attach to tier sides.

BAKE THE CAKE—a two-layer 10″ x 4″ round. Fill and ice with a smooth coat of chocolate buttercream. Place on rack and cover with chocolate poured fondant. When fondant has hardened, transfer to serving tray. Pipe tube 5 border.

MAKE YOUR OWN PATTERN for groom's initials. Transfer to cake top. Pipe outlines of letters with the tube 1 and Color Flow icing straight from the batch. Thin the icing and flow in the areas of the letters. Secure roses and leaves to cake on mounds of icing. Serve 1″ x 2″ pieces to 48 guests.

Allegro

As lovely as its name! Allegro makes full use of the fragile beauty of lattice. The trimly tailored construction is softened by lavish curves and subtle touches of color.

ASSEMBLE YOUR ACCESSORIES
Six 5" Grecian pillars
Two 10" Hexagon separator plates
Top ornament

Pipe trims ahead of time

PIPE LATTICE PIECES in royal icing. Tape patterns to stiff surface, tape wax paper over them, then pipe with tube 2. Edge lattice with same tube, then finish *curved edges only* with tube 14 scrolls.

PIPE FLOWERS in royal icing. Make tubes 217 and 224 drop flowers with tube 1 centers. Then make California poppies. Press foil just halfway into 1¼" lily nail, use stiff royal icing and tube 103. Touch center, pull icing over edge, straight across, then back to center for square, cupped petals. Smooth and fill centers with a damp brush. Trim tops off artificial stamens and brush with icing. Pipe a dot of icing in center of each flower and push in a few stamens. Mount some poppies on wire stems for between-tiers bouquet. Twist stems together, then frame with a ruffle of gathered tulle.

Prepare two-layer tiers

All tiers are baked in hexagon pans. Base tier is 15" x 4", middle tier is 12" x 4", top tier 9" x 3". Fill, ice and assemble with plates and pillars on cake board cut to hexagon shape. On base and top tiers, lightly mark position of lattice panels, using patterns.

Decorate the cake

PIPE SHELL BORDERS at top and bottom of all tiers, using tube 16. On base and top tiers, cover side corners with shells, also.

PIPE LEAVES on all sides of top and bottom tiers, using marks for lattice as guides. Do fern-like leaves with tube 2. Attach drop flowers in curves on lattice pieces for middle tier. Trim with tube 65 leaves. Secure prepared bouquet to center of separator plate.

Complete trim . . .

on the reception table. Attach lattice, working from top tier down. On top tier, pipe dots of icing on corner of tier and on separator plate. Set one lattice piece in position. Attach adjacent lattice piece, joining to first at corner. Continue to complete top tier. Edge corners and base of lattice with tube 13 shells.

On middle tier, pipe dots of icing on backs of lattice pieces and gently press to sides of tier. On bottom tier, secure lattice to sides just as you did for top tier. Edge with tube 13 shells.

Finish Allegro by attaching poppies to top and bottom tiers with dots of icing. Set ornament on top and trim with flowers. Serve two lower tiers to 116 guests.

CHAPTER FOUR

Masterpiece Cakes

that challenge the decorator

ALL THE EXQUISITE CAKES in this chapter are a joy and a challenge to you, the decorator. They're sure to arouse guests' admiration at the reception—and to delight the bride.

Browse through the pages to discover cakes decorated in foreign styles—Philippine, South African and English. Find others with unusual construction and unique trim. Most beautiful of all—a cake covered and adorned with satiny pulled sugar.

EXPERTS IN EACH TECHNIQUE have decorated these masterpieces. They share their knowledge with you in clear step-by-step pictures and directions. Do you enjoy a challenge to your skill? Study these pages and decorate a masterpiece of your own!

Sunrise *at right*

PHILIPPINE DECORATING is lavish and ornate—but really quick to do. Here is a cake decorated in the true Philippine style—but with an American difference. The flowers are not the traditional piped blossoms—instead they are lovely arrangements of silk flowers the bride and her attendants will treasure for years.

ASSEMBLE YOUR ACCESSORIES
Two 7″ separator plates
Four 7″ Corinthian pillars

Four Angelinos
Five 2¾″ Filigree bells
*Top plates from petite and
    regular-sized Heart bases*
Arch canopy trellis
Bridal couple figures
Silk flowers

Prepare trims in advance

FOR TOP ORNAMENT, glue trellis to larger top plate. Trim with flowers, twisting stems through trellis and adding loops of ribbon (see page 13). Glue bridal couple to plate.

MAKE BETWEEN-TIERS BOUQUET. Glue a bell to smaller top plate. Fill with a block of styrofoam, then arrange flowers, poufs of tulle and ribbon loops in it. Fill four bells with styrofoam for arrangements on square tier. Fill with flowers, ribbon loops and poufs.

DECORATE PILLARS. Assemble pillars with separator plates. Glue Angelinos to tops of pillars.

Prepare the tiers

All are two layers. You will need a 16″ x 4″ square tier, a 14″ x 4″ and a 6″ x 4″ round tier. Fill and ice. Philippine decorators traditionally use boiled icing to both cover and decorate the cake. Assemble the tiers on 20″ cake board with prepared pillars, plates and bouquet. Divide top edges of 6″ and 12″ tiers into sixths and transfer patterns. Divide each side of square base tier into sixths and mark at top edge.

Decorate the cake

DO TWO LOWER TIERS as a unit. At bottom of 14″ tier, pipe a large tube 21 curved shell just below the point where two curves of pattern above meet. Fill in with smaller curved shells to corresponding point between pattern curves. Pipe a second large curved shell. Continue around tier. Fill in pattern areas with tube 1 "sotas"—meandering curves and loops. Build up sotas a little heavier on top edge of cake. Edge sotas with tube 1 and an "e" motion. Center a tube 17 fleur-de-lis and star within each design. Edge separator plate with tube 14 shells.

ON BASE TIER, do bottom border with tube 18 curved shells. Trim with tube 16 stars and tube 13 scallops on cake board. Do top shell border with tube 18. Pipe tube 20 double drapes. "Hook" tube over top border as if starting a shell, then use lighter pressure to drop a string to next mark. Repeat procedure for lavish look. Continue around tier.

ON TOP TIER, pipe tube 18 rosettes for base border. Fill in marked patterns with tube 1 sotas, carrying right over edge to cover top of tier. Edge sotas with tube 1 scallops and tiny dots.

Now set ornament on cake top and secure flower arrangements on corners of base tier, piping a mound of icing below each bell. Sunrise is just breathtaking! Serve two lower tiers to 220 guests.

Las Cadenas

FLAMBOYANT, DRAMATIC, yet completely dainty and delicate—that's the Philippine method of decorating. Here we show it at its most traditional in a wedding cake crowned with an exuberant "fountain" of flowers.

In the Philippine method, a pound cake recipe is used for the cake and tiers are covered with boiled icing. Crumbs are brushed off, then the icing is applied directly to the tiers without a preliminary crumb coating. All borders and trims are piped in this icing, too. You'll find that boiled icing flows very easily from the tube and makes the heavy borders easy to pipe. Perhaps you'll use this icing for trim on all your cakes. We recommend it for its speed and ease.

PROPORTIONS OF PHILLIPPINE cakes are very different from cakes in the Wilton-American style. Pillars are taller, tiers are smaller, for an exaggerated effect. Often a top ornament or bouquet is almost as tall as the entire cake. Borders are heavy, ornate and sculptural. Skillfully piped flowers are used in abundance and ribbon trim adds a special satiny shine.

You'll enjoy decorating a wedding cake in the true Philippine style. Perhaps you'll adopt many of the techniques to incorporate into your own personal style of decorating. You'll find they are quick, easy and very effective.

Pipe the flowers

Study page 12 for the "upside down" method of Phillippine flower making. You'll find it fast and fun. For Las Cadenas you will need daisies (shown on page 12), Damas de Noche, roses and rosebuds. *All flowers are piped in royal icing,* using very light pressure. Almost all flowers start with a pistil, or center, piped in yellow royal icing on a florists' wire stem.

Before you start, weight a cake rack on one end so you can hang the flowers on the extending end of the rack to dry.

ROSEBUD

DAMA DE NOCHE

ROSE

DAISY. Pipe these just as described on page 12, using tube 7 for pistils, tube 1 for stamens and tube 81 for petals. Hang upside down to dry.

ROSEBUD. Pipe pistils with tube 5. Use tube 103 and spatula-striped cone. Holding end of wire with pistil at bottom, touch tube, wide side at base of pistil and tip almost parallel. Turn stem as you press, increasing angle of tube as you twirl. Stop pressure and break off. Dry on rack, upside down.

DAMA DE NOCHE. A tiny Philippine flower that opens at night. Make pistils with tube 5. Holding wire with pistil upside down touch widest part of tube 55 to pistil, squeeze lightly, stop, and draw away to point. Make six petals on each flower. Dry upside down.

ROSE. Pipe pistils (not shown) with tube 5. Hold upside down and twirl a tube 103 ribbon down around pistil, keeping tube parallel to pistil. Add three closed petals, then five open petals with tube at 45°angle to pistil. Hang upside down on rack to dry.

SPRAYS FOR FOUNTAIN. Take a 12″ length of fine white florists' wire and bend tiny hook on one end. With royal icing and tube 13, pipe tiny stars on wire every half inch, starting with unhooked tip and working for two-thirds the length of the wire. Touch tube to wire, squeeze very lightly and pull away. Hang the wire by its hook on cake rack to dry. Repeat for about two dozen sprays. When thoroughly dry, twist the base of the wires together, bind with floral tape and hang upside down.

Form flowers into sprays

Make twelve pink and twelve white bows of ¼″ wide ribbon. Fold ribbon into two loops and bind with a 4″ length of fine florists' wire. Make four large bouquets for base tier, each with two daisies, three roses, four rosebuds and many Damas de Noche. Twist stems together with wires of two bows. Bind with floral tape. Make six little bouquets for top tier, each with a daisy, a rosebud, several damas de noche and two bows.

Prepare the tiers

Bake two-layer tiers, one 6″ round, the other 10″ round. Fill and ice with boiled icing. Finished height of each tier is about 3½″. Assemble with 7″ Corinthian pillars and 8″ separator plates on foil-covered cake board. (Philippine decorators need to improvise their own pillars from dowels and gum paste, so having plastic pillars makes the work go more quickly.)

MEASURE AND MARK tiers. Divide top tier into eighths and mark at top edge. Make a second series of marks 2″ above base, midway between marks above.

Divide bottom tier into twelfths and mark at top edge.

Decorate the cake

ON BASE TIER, pipe large zigzag garlands from mark to mark in "V" shapes with tube 48, making them about 2″ deep. Pipe garlands in one continous motion, extending ends above cake edge to give them extra sweep and drama. Add a large tube 22 star atop each of the extensions. Finish garlands with tube 1 dots.

When garlands are complete, pipe a frame of two rows of tube 4 dots directly below them and add a large tube 22 star beneath point of each "V". Edge tier with a bottom border of tube 22 standing curves and with same tube, pipe a large star between each curve on cake board.

Now pipe the "sotas" or cornelli-like lacework within the garlands. Use tube 1 and pipe tiny curls, "v's" and "c's" of icing in all directions, very close together, starting and stopping over and over again. Fill garlands and top of tier up to separator plate with sotas for a lace-encrusted look. Pipe tube 1 dots around separator plate. On plate, pipe a curved line of tube 1 dots between pillars. Add tube 22 stars around pillars.

TOP TIER. Decorate in similar fashion to bottom tier, using same tubes. Make "V"-shaped garlands, using marks as guides. Pipe accent dots on top of curves. Measure an inch in from top edge of tier and pipe a scalloped frame of tube 1 dots. Fill in up to scallops with sotas.

Add flower trim

Push fountain into center of top tier on mound of icing. Hold for a few minutes to set. Push six small bouquets into cake around fountain. Secure a small cluster of flowers on separator plate. Push four larger bouquets into bottom tier, lining up with pillars. Carefully curve fountain wires in cascade effect.

Las Cadenas is dramatically beautiful. Both tiers will serve 64 guests.

Overture

THE TIERS OF OVERTURE are trimmed with perfectly piped sprays of lily of the valley. There's a surprise within the arched pillars—a miniature replica of the bridal cake to freeze for the first anniversary celebration.

ASSEMBLE ACCESSORIES. *For main cake:* Arched pillar set; four 5″ Grecian pillars; two 10″ separator plates, Kneeling cherub fountain; Heart base; Bridal couple. *For replica cake:* Round mini-tier set; two Small doves; Petite couple.

Prepare the tiers

FOR MAIN CAKE, bake, fill and ice two-layer tiers—16″ x 4″, 12″ x 4″ and 8″ x 3″. Assemble with plates and pillars. Divide base tier into twelfths and mark near bottom. Divide middle and top tiers into twelfths, mark at top edge.

FOR REPLICA CAKE, bake and ice single-layer tiers in mini-tier pans. Assemble on ruffle-trimmed cake board. Measure and mark the tiers just as you did for main cake.

Decorate main cake

DO TWO LOWER TIERS as a unit. On middle tier, pipe groups of long tube 68 leaves curving from top of tier down side. Pipe tube 2 stems, then add tiny blossoms with tube 79. (See page 63.)

ON BASE TIER, pipe a group of tube 68 leaves at each mark. Add tube 2 stems and tube 79 blossoms. Pipe shell borders on both tiers with tube 22.

ON TOP TIER, pipe a tube 22 bottom shell border. Starting on tier top and extending down side, pipe tube 68 leaves, tube 2 stems and tube 79 blossoms. Trim cherub figure with tube 68 leaves in royal icing.

Decorate tiny replica cake

This little cake is trimmed just like the main cake, but with smaller tubes. Use tube 66 for leaves, tube 1 for stems and tube 81 for flowers. Do all borders with tube 17.

Add finishing touches

On replica cake, drop tube 1 strings and loops from top tier. Place within arched pillars. Attach doves and petite couple. On main cake, set cherub within upper pillars. Drop tube 2 strings and loops from top tier, using curves on separator plate as guide. Serve three tiers of main cake to 216 guests.

ON THIS ALL-WHITE bridal cake, the dramatic surprise is a sparkling fountain—the cascades of water playing *from the top* of the tiers.

ASSEMBLE ACCESSORIES: 12″ x 4″ styrofoam cake dummy; four 10¼″ Roman columns; two 12″ round separator plates; Kolor-Flo fountain; Ornament; sixteen 1″ Filigree bells.

Do trims in advance

FOR ROSES, use royal icing and tubes 102 and 104. Pipe spikes on backs of most flowers.

FOR FOUNTAIN TIER, cut a 10″ circle from center of dummy with a sharp knife, leaving a shell. Line with foil, then attach to a 12″ cake circle. Cut an opening at back of shell near bottom. Insert fountain, extending wire through opening. Ice shell with royal icing. Divide into sixteenths and mark midway on side and at top edge.

Prepare the two-layer tiers

Bake, fill and ice 14″ x 4″ and 18″ x 4″ square tiers. Form 18″ tier from two 10″ and two 8″ two-layer squares. (See diagram, page 38.) Assemble on 22″ cake board. Divide each side of 18″ tier into fourths and mark midway on side. Divide sides of 14″ tier into eighths, mark at top and midway on side.

Decorate the cake

DO TWO LOWER TIERS as a unit. On 14″ tier, pipe a tube 320 reverse shell border at base. Drop guidelines and pipe tube 16 zigzag garlands. Attach bells to points of every other garland, then add tube 3 string and bows. Drop double string drapes from top edge, then pipe corresponding scallops on tier top with tube 3 bulbs.

ON BASE TIER, drop guidelines and pipe tube 352 garlands. Drape with tube 4 strings and bows.

DECORATE FOUNTAIN TIER in royal icing. Pipe a tube 14 reverse shell bottom border. Pipe garlands with same tube from mark to mark, drape with tube 3 string and bows. Pipe tube 3 double string drapes.

TRIM ALL TIERS with roses, pushing spiked flowers into sides of base tier. Set ornament within pillars and circle with roses. Plug in the fountain and admire the sound and light. Crystal serves 260.

Crystal

THE SOUTH AFRICAN LACEWORK STYLE is notable for its flamboyant wings that make a cake look almost airborne. Also unmistakeable is the delicacy of execution. Though the wings are large and showy, the fragile lattice and lace is piped precisely with the smallest of round tubes.

Eleanor Rielander a resident of Johannesburg, South Africa, created this showpiece cake in the Wilton Book Division's decorating room as a beautiful example of the South African lace work style. Mrs. Rielander is an accomplished decorator who teaches cake decorating at the technical college in her home city. She frequently serves as a judge at cake shows and has made several trips to the United States and other countries to teach this unique method.

The lacework

The large lace wings are the hallmark of this style. Often, the fine lattice work is piped over a curved surface for dimensional effect. Special nails are used for this—or the decorator may resort to ingenuity. An example: the smaller ball in the cake at right was piped over a ping pong ball, the columns over a curtain rod! Mrs. Rielander's royal icing for lacework is especially strong.

MAKE ONLY AS MUCH ICING as you will use immediately—this icing will not hold its texture. Confectioners' sugar should be sieved until completely lump free, and the egg should be at least several days old. Use a small porcelain or glass bowl—plastic often holds grease. Aluminum may discolor the icing. Place a teaspoon or two of the egg white in the container and beat with a small spatula until frothy. Add a pinch of cream of tartar, then the sugar, a tablespoon at a time, beating by hand until fluffy. When icing peaks on the spatula, it is ready. Keep covered with a damp cloth to prevent crusting. For piping, use a very small paper cone.

The gum paste flowers

The petals are rolled until they are nearly transparent. This is accomplished by greasing the rolling surface with solid white vegetable shortening, then wiping it off until only the merest film remains. The petals are cut using cutters of Mrs. Rielander's design, shaped briefly by hand, then delicately brushed with powdered chalk. Dry the petals a few minutes on a curved surface, such as a wooden spoon handle, just until they hold their shape. Next assemble with egg white, shape to curves and dry thoroughly. Prop the petals with wisps of cotton to hold their shape.

Covering the cake

Cakes to be entered in important shows are still covered the classic way; first with marzipan, then royal icing. In recent years, however, rolled fondant has often been used for wedding cakes for ease and quickness.

The showpiece cake

The tiers are 3″ high, baked of fruit cake. Base tier is 12″ square, middle tier 9″ square. Measuring in 1″ from each corner, trim off the corners of each tier. The top tier is 6″ round. Cover tiers in rolled fondant. The top tier rests on a 7″ clear plate. Clear pillars are 3″ high. The frangipani (plumeria) flowers are skillfully made of gum paste. Pipe all the lace pieces with tube 000 and royal icing, piping main lines with tube 1 for added strength.

Assemble the wings on the top tier *with care.* Pipe a line of icing on the wing where it will touch the tier, place on tier, then reinforce with a few dots of icing on either side. Hold until set. After seven of the wings are in place, attach the small ball, then add the eighth wing. Now position the half-ball and top ball. Attach butterflies last.

Use the recipes in Chapter Nine for marzipan, rolled fondant and gum paste. See patterns in Appendix.

For a full chapter with many pictures on the South African style, see The Wilton Way of Cake Decorating, Volume Two.

A **S**outh **A**frican *showpiece*

Love Story

A WEDDING CAKE that comes straight from a fairy tale! The romantic bride and groom who meet within the pillars are fashioned from gum paste—the following pages tell just how to do it. The tiers are lavished with delicate gum paste blossoms and a hand-fashioned double ring ornament crowns the cake. Love Story is a young bride's dream cake.

ASSEMBLE YOUR ACCESSORIES
Arched pillar tier set
Two 10" Hexagon separator plates
Six 5" Grecian pillars
Flower garden cutter set

Make trims in advance

THE FLOWERS are made from gum paste, using the forget-me-not and violet cutters. You will need a great many, but the cutters make them quick to do. Review the instruction book that comes with the Flower garden cutter set, then make the flowers. Tint gum paste (recipe page 164), roll out very thin and cut the flowers. Lay on foam toweling and press each petal from edge to center to curl. Dry, then pipe tube 2 stamens.

Mount about 300 violets on fine florists' wire stems. Mount about 25 forget-me-nots on wire stems. Remaining flowers will form clusters.

MAKE DOUBLE RING ornament for top of cake. Cut a 10" gum paste strip, ⅜" wide, and set on edge to form a 3" circle. Cut an 8" strip ¼" wide and form into a 2½" circle. Dry. Trim rings with tube 1s beading and zigzags.

Cut a 4½" circle from 1" thick styrofoam and ice with royal icing. Pipe tube 14 fleurs-de-lis around sides and edge with stars piped with same tube. Secure rings upright on this base with royal

icing. Tape about two dozen wired forget-me-nots into a cluster with floral tape and insert in base behind rings.

MAKE HEART BOUQUET for between pillars. You will need six gum paste hearts. Cut from gum paste, using a 1" heart cutter. Cut one heart, dip a 5" length of florists' wire in egg white and lay on heart. Dry. Cut second heart, brush first heart with egg white and join the two. Dry, then edge with tube 1 beading. Tape into spray. Ice a 3" styrofoam half-ball. Tape wired violets into several sprays and insert into half-ball along with heart spray.

MAKE FLOWERY BASE for bridal couple. Ice a 10" styrofoam circle, 1" thick and edge with tube 13 shells. Make many sprays of violets by taping stems together. Insert in base, keeping flowers low in front and gradually rising to about a 3" height in back.

Prepare the tiers

Bake, fill and ice the two-layer tiers—16" x 4" round, 12" x 4" round and 9" x 3" hexagon. Assemble on arched pillar tier set with 5" pillars and plates.

On base tier, using pillars below as guides, divide into sixths and mark at top edge. Divide middle tier into twenty-fourths and mark 1" up from base. Divide top edge of tier into twelfths.

Decorate the cake

DO TWO LOWER TIERS as a unit. On 12" tier pipe a tube 17 shell border at base. Top with tube 13 strings. Drop triple strings with tube 13 from marks on top of tier, leaving space between each set of strings. Edge top of tier with tube 17 shells. Edge separator plate with tube 13.

ON BASE TIER, pipe six arches on sides. The upright columns are

done with tube 32. Line them up with the tops of the arched pillars below. Pipe the scrolls above with tube 18. Pipe tube 18 shells to complete bottom border. Do top border with same tube.

MAKE FLOWER CLUSTERS Pipe a mound of icing extending over top edge of 12" tier and halfway down side, between two sets of triple strings. Press in flowers, placing larger ones in center. Attach smaller flowers on outside of mound with dots of icing.

Continue making flower clusters, six on 12" tier and six on 16" tier.

ON TOP TIER, pipe upright columns at each corner with tube 32. Add two scrolls at top of each with tube 16, then center scrolls with a tube 16 star. Using same tube, pipe a shell border at base and a star border on top edge of tier. Finish with a tube 16 fleur-de-lis in center of each side.

Assemble the wedding cake

Center flower base on base plate of Arched Pillar set. Attach bridal couple by pushing wires on feet into styrofoam. Set pillars in place, then position two lower tiers on pillars.

Secure heart bouquet to hexagon separator plate with icing. Set 5" pillars in position and add top tier. Pipe a mound of icing on top of tier and attach double ring ornament. Two lower tiers of Love Story serve 196 guests.

For directions on making the romantic bridal couple, please turn the page.

A Fairy tale wedding ornament

The magic of gum paste creates the beautiful bride and her dashing Prince Charming. The figures are molded, then dressed in colorful gum paste clothing. Before you start, study the instructions in the booklet that comes with the People Molds. Then make a recipe of gum paste and begin your adventure! The handsome couple will be in perfect proportion and perfectly beautiful.

Mold and dress the bride

Read the directions for modeling and dressing a standing figure in the People Mold book. Here we give you only the details that are specific to this costume. The Appendix gives the pattern for skirt.

DRAPE THE BLUE SASH after the skirt has dried on the figure. Use a little very soft gum paste that has not been stiffened with additional sugar. Make your own pattern by cutting out a rectangle ¾" x 4½" from light cardboard. Make a second pattern for streamer by cutting a long triangle, 2½" at base with each long side 7½". Cut off 1" from point.

Roll the soft gum paste very thin and cut the sash. Brush a little egg white around top of skirt and drape the sash around the hips. Cut the streamer. Brush egg white on skirt just below closing of sash. Pleat top of streamer and press to skirt. Arrange in graceful folds. Add the arms and the figure is almost complete.

THE FINISHING TOUCHES are the most fun! Embroider the dress with tube 1, starting at hem. Pipe tube ls hair and necklace.

MAKE TINY ROSE on the end of an icing-covered wire. Hand-model petals from little balls of gum paste, attaching with egg white. Cut ⅛" wide gum paste strips, form loops and streamers and attach to stem with egg white while still wet. When dry, secure to hand with royal icing.

FOR CORONET, form a little string of gum paste into a circlet, 1" in diameter. Dry, then trim with tube ls.

FOR VEIL, fold a 24" x 10" piece of fine tulle in half to 12" x 10". Gather 10" folded edge and secure to hair with royal icing. Attach crown with icing.

Mold and dress Prince Charming

Mold the figure following directions for standing figure in People Mold booklet. Legs and lower body are molded in green gum paste, other parts in flesh color. Mold an extra head and upper torso to help in draping the cape.

DRESS THE FIGURE in jacket and boots as described in booklet. Add cuffs to boot by cutting a ½" x 2⅞" strip, moistening long edge with egg white and attaching to boot.

After trimming jacket with gold strips, add the sash. Cut a ½" x 8" strip, apply a little egg white to shoulder and drape wet sash around figure. Secure with more egg white at right side and trim ends.

CUT CAPE from pattern in Appendix. Roll lower edge with modeling stick 2 to make folds. Lay extra upper torso face down, form a pleat in center of cape, and place on back of extra torso. Use cotton balls to preserve folds while drying. When cape is dry, turn over and pipe royal icing fleurs-de-lis with tube ls.

FOR CUFFS cut 2½" x ½" strips of gum paste. Brush one edge with egg white and attach to sleeve. When dry, trim with a ⅛" wide gold strip of gum paste.

ATTACH CAPE to shoulders with small pieces of gum paste dipped in egg white. Cut a ¼" strip for cape strap and attach. Trim strap with tube ls design in royal icing. Make brooches for cape strap from flattened small balls of gum paste. Attach to ends of strap with egg white and impress with tube 26. Finally, trim sleeve and boot cuffs with tube 1 cornelli and royal icing. Prince Charming is complete!

Mount the couple on the flowery base as described on page 97.

To learn much more about creating charming figures and flowers in gum paste, see The Wilton Way of Cake Decorating, Volume Two.

Baroque

A magnificent and most unusual wedding cake! Gum paste baskets filled with dainty gum paste blossoms adorn the tiers. Lavishly piped scrolls of icing set them off. Decorate Baroque for a bride who loves fine design.

ASSEMBLE YOUR ACCESSORIES
Australian basket nails
Flower garden cutter set
12" round separator plate
11" square separator plate
Four 5" Grecian pillars
Top ornament

Make gum paste flowers

Tint equal amounts of gum paste in three pastel shades. Review the booklet that comes with the flower cutters for procedures.

Use violet cutter for larger flowers to fill between-tiers basket. Use forget-me-not cutter for smaller flowers. Cut many flowers from each color.

Press each petal from tip to center with modeling stick, then dry. Pipe tube 1 centers. Mount larger flowers on wire stems.

Make the baskets

Use basket nail as form. Roll out gum paste thinly, and cut a strip 6½" x 1⅝". Make grooves ⅛" apart with edge of thin cardboard. Dust nail with cornstarch and set in styrofoam block. Carefully smooth strip around nail, joining ends with egg white. Dry overnight and remove from nail.

Roll out gum paste ⅛" thick and set basket on it to make an impression for base. Set basket aside, cut out base. Brush edge with egg white and set basket on base to attach. Dry. Cut three ⅛" strips about 6½" long, brush with egg white and wrap around basket. Add a ring made by cutting a circle with tube 1A and removing center with tube 2A. When basket is thoroughly dry, insert a small piece of styrofoam, securing with royal icing, and arrange bouquet of wired blossoms.

Make four half-baskets the same way, but cover only half of nail.

Prepare the tiers

Bake and fill 14" x 4", 10" x 4" and 6" x 3" square, two-layer tiers. Ice very smoothly with buttercream. Assemble on a foil-covered cake board with plates and pillars. Transfer patterns to tiers.

Decorate the cake

PIPE SHELL BORDERS. Use tube 18 for base tier, tube 16 for center tier and tube 14 for top tier. Edge separator plate with tube 13.

STARTING AT TOP, pipe all scrolls and trim on tiers with tube 16, then over-pipe with tube 14. Drop string guidelines to mark position of garlands on base and top tiers. Pipe ends of garlands with tube 13, then pipe a heavy curve with tube 12. Press in small flowers.

ATTACH HALF-BASKETS to sides of 10" tier on mounds of icing. Pipe a large mound of icing above each basket and press in flowers. Trim ornament with flowers and set on cake. Place basket within pillars. Two lower tiers of Baroque serve 160 guests.

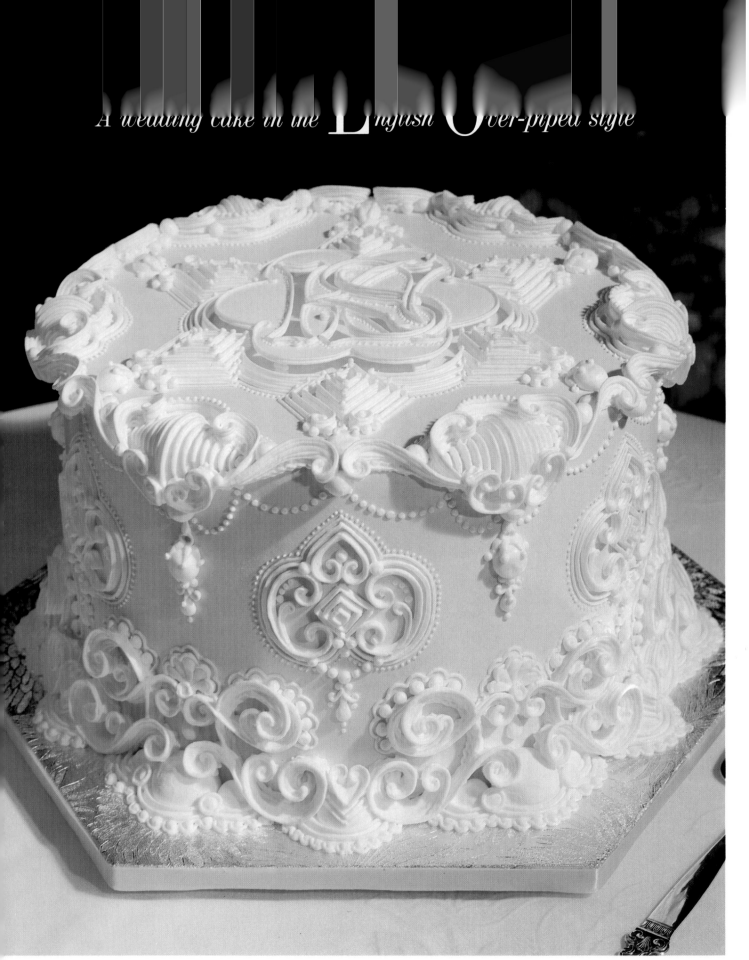

THE OVER-PIPED STYLE is distinguished by line-upon-line of curving, accurate piping that results in a formal, ornate, very sculptural cake. Sometimes called the Lambeth style, after its best-known practitioner, this style was perfected by many skilled English decorators in the nineteenth and present century.

Cakes in the over-piped style have an unusually lofty proportion. Wedding cakes are designed in several tiers, or, as in this beautiful example, in a single tier. All demand careful, skilled piping to achieve the built-up effect.

Michael Nitzsche, an expert in the style, has designed and decorated this impressive centerpiece. Here we show you, step-by-step, how to re-create it.

Prepare the cake

English wedding cakes are made of fruit cake, covered first with marzipan, then royal icing. These coverings keep the cake moist and fresh for a long period and provide a perfectly smooth surface for the intricate decoration. For marzipan and icing, use the recipes in

Chapter Nine.

BAKE SUFFICIENT LAYERS of fruit cake in 10″ round pans to achieve a final height of 6″. We baked two layers, each about 2½″ high. (Marzipan and icing add extra height.) Brush one layer with apricot glaze, fill with a circle of marzipan, brush marzipan with glaze, then add second layer. Make sure that the top of cake is completely level. Attach a cardboard cake circle, same size as the cake, to its top with royal icing. Fill in any cracks or holes by pressing in bits of marzipan. Now flip over the cake so the cake circle is on the bottom.

ROLL OUT A BALL of marzipan to a circle about ⅜″ thick and a little larger than the diameter of cake. Brush the top of the cake (this was the bottom) with hot apricot glaze and place cake on marzipan circle, glazed side down. Press gently, then cut off excess marzipan with a sharp knife.

FORM A LONG CYLINDER from marzipan and roll out to a width slightly larger than height of cake.

With a sharp knife straighten one

long edge. Turn cake upright, brush side with apricot glaze, set cake on its side on the marzipan strip, bottom touching straight edge of marzipan. Roll it like a wheel to cover side, patting into place. Butt seam smoothly, then trim off excess marzipan on top edge. Pat entire cake to smooth, then let harden 48 hours. This will prevent the oil in the marzipan from seeping through the finished icing.

ICE SMOOTHLY with royal icing, dry, then cover with a second coat. Set cake on a foil-covered hexagon cake board, measuring 16″ from point to opposite point.

Decorate the top

Here directions for top and side trim are given separately, but you will find yourself working on both almost simultaneously, as you allow piped lines to crust. Remember, *complete no more than two lines of piping* before allowing icing to harden. All trim is piped in royal icing.

TRANSFER ALL PATTERNS to cake, lining up as picture shows. Design your own initials to fit inside top

Please turn the page

plaque, then do plaque in the "run-in" (Color Flow) method. After drying, outline edge with tube 2, then outline the letters with tube 1. Over-pipe with a second tube 1 line and edge with tube 1 dots. Pipe plaque supports with four superimposed lines of tube 2.

NOW FOR THE OVER-PIPING! First outline outer edge of diamonds with tube 2. Over-pipe four times with the same tube, then add two pipings with tube 1. Within diamond pipe a second smaller and higher one, first with six lines of tube 2, then with two tube 1 lines. Pipe a third tiny diamond with seven lines of tube 2, and two lines of tube 1.

Pipe inner scallops and frame outer sides of diamonds with five over-piped tube 2 lines and two tube 1 lines. Move out and overpipe four tube 2 lines and one tube 1 line. Move out again and pipe a tube 3 line over-piped with tubes 2 and 1. Pipe a fourth outline with tube 2, then tube 1. Finally pipe a tube 1 line to complete design. Edge curves and top corners with tube 1 dots. Add large "pearls" with tube 4.

FOR UPSTANDING CURVES on top edge, use only tube 2. Pipe 15 short, evenly spaced lines. Starting with second line, and ending with the next-to-the last line, over-pipe each. Continue until center line is over-piped seven times.

FRAME THE EDGE with curved scrolls. First pipe them with zigzags done with tube 13. Over-pipe with a tube 13 line, then over-pipe with tubes 4, 3 and 2. Add curves of tube 2 "pearls" and a large pearl, where scrolls join, with tube 4. Between side designs pipe a large tube 4 pearl and trim with tube 2 curves and dots.

Decorate the side and base

OUTLINE CURVED SIDE SCROLLS with tube 1. Pipe inner curves with tube 3, over-pipe with tube 1. Edge with tube 1 dots. Outline diamond shapes with tube 3, overpipe with two lines of tube 1. Pipe second diamond within first with tube 3, over-pipe with tube 3 and two lines of tube 1. Pipe smallest diamond with tubes 3, 3, 3, 2, 2 and 1. Pipe tube 2 pearls, bulbs and curves.

FOR BASE TRIM, start with a large tube 7 pearl. Pipe a tube 3 heart on top of it. Do curved scrolls with tube 13 zigzags, over-pipe with tube 13 lines, then with tubes 3, 3, 2 and 2. Add a fan of tube 2 bulbs at top center of design, pipe tube 3 dots above side curves, then tube 1 scallops.

IN CENTER OF BASE design, pipe a tube 7 pearl with a tube 3 pearl on each side. Frame pearls at base with tube 4 over-piped with tubes 3 and 2, then frame a second time with tube 3 over-piped with tube 2. Finish with tube 2 pearls and tiny tube 1 strings on cake board. Over-pipe hearts with tubes 2 and 1. Pipe dots of icing on plaque supports and position plaque. Serve your beautiful over-piped masterpiece to 48 guests.

For other magnificent English over-piped cakes, read The Wilton Way of Cake Decorating, Volume Two.

Directions on next page

TRULY FASCINATING, PULLED SUGAR is an art that produces spectacular decorating effects. Here Norman Wilton shows you just how to create a breathtaking pulled sugar wedding cake.

EQUIPMENT YOU'LL NEED

40- to 60-gauge brass wire screen
Marble slab about 2' x 3'
Canvas strip about 3' x 14"
Electric heater (guard removed)
Metal candy scraper
Candy thermometer
Scissors
Small leaf mold

Prepare the cake

Bake and fill the two-layer tiers— 14", 10" and 6". Cover with rolled fondant and assemble with 8" plates and 5" iridescent pillars.

Cook the sugar

To decorate a cake of this size you need two recipes for a yield of 10 pounds. If you are a beginner, we suggest you work with just one recipe at a time. With the first recipe, do steps 1 through 9. Then complete remaining steps with second recipe. Pulled sugar will droop and lose its gloss in hot, humid weather, so *do this decorating only on a dry, clear day.*

PULLED SUGAR RECIPE

  10 cups granulated cane sugar
  2½ cups water
  1 teaspoon cream of tartar

Grease marble slab with lard. Add water to sugar and mix by hand until mixture is smooth and all lumps have dissolved. Add cream of tartar and cook at highest heat to 312°F, washing down the sides of the pan often with a wet pastry brush to avoid crystals. Pour out on greased slab.

1. Let cool a few minutes; then with a scraper, begin flipping sugar around edges, turning it over on all sides to keep it from sticking and to allow it to cool evenly. As you work quickly, you'll see the sugar start to cool and begin to hold together.

2. Keep flipping the edges of the sugar and work it into a mass.

3. Let cool to pulling temperature, similar to that of pulling taffy.

4. When you can safely touch the sugar with your hands, pull and stretch it to make it pliable. As you start to pull, the sugar will loose its opaque quality and become more transparent. After you've worked the sugar, place it on the mesh screen in front of the heater to keep it at an even temperature.

Divide the batch in two before placing it in front of heater. When one batch seems somewhat stiffer, place it closer to the heater and work with the other batch. Always fold ends of sugar inward to keep heat concentrated throughout.

Make ribbons for tiers

5. Cut off a piece of sugar about 7" x 2" and place it on the canvas strip.

6. Begin pulling and stretching sugar, lengthening it as you work.

7. As you pull and stretch the sugar, it will acquire sheen and gloss. Now fold ribbon over, side by side, doubling its width.

8. Re-pull and stretch again. Work fast before sugar becomes stiff.

9. When you have enough length to wrap a tier, cut off the uneven ends and wrap tier from front to back, overlapping at seam. Where the ends meet will be the back of the cake. Do the same to wrap all three tiers, covering each twice.

Make ruffle trims

10. To make the base ruffles for the bottom and middle tiers, cut off a piece of sugar just as you did for the ribbons. Pull and stretch it on the canvas. When it's about the length you desire, cut off the uneven ends, turn piece over, (shinier candy is underneath) and pinch ribbon to ruffle.

11. When strip is completely ruffled, wrap around base of tier from front to back. If one piece of ruffle is not enough, make more and piece.

Add more trims

12. Cut off a 7″ long, thin piece of sugar, pull and stretch it on the canvas. Cut it into 6″ pieces and attach as garlands to top tier.

13. Cut off a long thin piece of sugar. Roll it back and forth on the canvas to form a rope twist.

14. While still soft and pliable, wrap rope around base of top tier.

Make lavish bows

15. Now make many loops. Cut off a long thin piece of sugar, pull and stretch it on the canvas. Cut into 6″ long pieces and fold over thumb, pressing ends together to form loops. Set on ends to harden. To make bow for between tiers, place a 3″ circle of unpulled sugar on plate. Touch ends of loops to heater, then attach to circle working from center out.
To trim ornament, press a strip of unpulled sugar around base. Heat ends of loops to attach to strip.

16. For bows on tier sides, make a flat circle of unpulled sugar about 3″ in diameter. Heat to attach to tier. Next, heat ends of loops and attach to circle, working from outer edge in. Repeat for two more bows.

Make flowering vine

17. Cut a long thin piece of sugar and roll it on the canvas to form a rope. Wind the rope around a long stick or broom handle, and let stand a few minutes until sugar is cool enough to hold curves.

18. Pull off stick and place around top of middle tier. Heat a few tiny pieces of sugar to secure to the separator plate at several points.

19. To make flowers, pinch off a small piece of sugar. Hold it in your left hand, press with your right thumb to form a cupped petal. Make five petals and press bases together to form a flower. Next, pull off a small piece of sugar and roll around base of artificial stamens to insert in flower center. To make leaves, cut off a piece of sugar and press into small leaf mold to shape. Touch to heater to place on cake.

Serve your glittering showpiece to 156 guests. The delicious pulled sugar will shatter as you cut it—serve some to each guest.

CHAPTER FIVE

Wedding Cakes Small in size... Big in appeal

In this chapter, we present a bouquet of petite bridal cakes planned for smaller receptions. All serve fewer than 100 guests. Every one is just as pretty and impressive as a larger cake. They're trimmed with all the lovely symbols of romance—ruffles and bows, hearts and flowers, beguiling cupids and dainty lattice.

Leaf through the pages—if you find a cake design you love, but need more servings, just increase the size of the tiers. Or add another tier at the base of the cake.

Hearts and flowers

A charming little bridal cake is linked by a lacy stairway with a cake for the groom! There's a bonus for the busy decorator, too. While the tableau looks very important, Hearts and Flowers is quick to decorate. Tiers are covered in satiny poured fondant, fast drop flowers are used in border effects and the bouquet is fashioned of lovely silk flowers.

ASSEMBLE YOUR ACCESSORIES
Harvest cherub separator set
2¾" Filigree bell
Top plate from Petite heart base
Frolicking cherub
Filigree stairway and bridge
Silk flowers

Do trims in advance

Pipe drop flowers in royal icing and tubes 132 and 225. Use varied tints of pink. Add tube 2 centers and dry.

Glue bell to top plate to form vase. Insert a block of styrofoam, attaching with royal icing. Arrange silk flowers by sticking stems into styrofoam.

Prepare the tiers

FOR BRIDE'S CAKE, bake and fill a two-layer 14" x 4" round and an 8" x 3" two-layer round.

FOR GROOM'S CAKE, bake and fill two-layer tiers, 10" x 4" round and 6" x 3" heart shape.

Ice all tiers with buttercream. Let icing crust then cover with poured fondant—white for the bride's cake, chocolate and pastel pink for the groom's cake. Assemble both cakes.

On bride's cake, divide base tier into twelfths and mark 1" up from bottom. Press a 2" heart cookie cutter into icing to form side designs. On top tier, divide in tenths and mark 1" up from bottom for garlands. On groom's cake, divide base tier into twelfths and mark 1" up from bottom.

Decorate the bride's cake

ON BASE TIER, pipe a tube 20 bottom shell border. Pipe heart designs with tube 16, then link with curved shells. Edge separator plate with tube 14. Attach a cluster of drop flowers to each heart.

ON TOP TIER, pipe a tube 16 bottom shell border. Drop guidelines from mark to mark with same tube, then press in drop flowers in garlands. Top garlands with tube 2 bows.

Decorate the groom's cake

On base tier, pipe a bottom shell border with tube 16. Drop guidelines from mark to mark, then pipe garlands with tube 16. Cover with drop flowers. On top tier, pipe a thick line of icing around base with tube 20. Press in drop flowers to form border.

ATTACH BRIDGE TO STAIRWAY and join the two cakes. Set bouquet within pillars and cherub on bridge. Add a scattering of drop flowers on stairway. Serve lower tier of bride's cake to 92 guests. Groom's cake serves 60.

Cupid

Dainty details, meticulously piped, create a polished little showpiece. A cherub plays his flute atop the heart-shaped tier.

Pipe flowers in advance
Use royal icing and tube 225. Pipe tube 2 centers and dry.

Prepare the tiers
Base tier is 14″ x 4″, upper tier a 9″ x 3″ heart shape. Bake, fill and ice with buttercream. Assemble on serving tray.

Divide base tier in sixths and mark 1″ up from bottom. Lightly mark the sides with a pattern press. Mark same design in center of heart tier. Make double scallop pattern for top of base tier. (There are twelve scallops.) Mark on tier. Mark double heart outline on top tier, following shape of cake.

Decorate the cake
DO CORNELLI FIRST with tube 1. Fill in area within double heart pattern on top tier, then completely cover sides of tier. Fill in area within double scallops on base tier. Fill all pattern press designs with cornelli.

ON BASE TIER, pipe tube 21 curved shells around bottom. Outline side designs with circular motions of tube 14. Do top shell border with tube 19. Drop tube 3 string on lower side of tier. On tier top, outline double scallops with tube 3. Border with tube 1 dots.

ON TOP TIER, pipe tube 17 shell borders at bottom and top. Outline double heart design with tube 3, then border with tube 1 dots. Outline center design with tube 14 and circular motion.

ACCENT CAKE with flowers and tube 65 leaves. Trim cherub fountain with flowers and set on cake. Cupid is enchanting! Serve lower tier to 92 guests.

Rosy Dream

Directions, page 112

Sentimental

The most beguiling love cake you could create for a small wedding celebration! Every inch is sweetly feminine from the ruffled, bow-tied tiers to the flounced top ornament.

ASSEMBLE ACCESSORIES: 16″ and 10″ plates, a 6½″ column and four glue-on legs (from Tall tier stand); 4″ Filigree heart; plate from Petite heart base; Cake corer.

Pipe the flowers

Use royal icing and tubes 15, 225 and 131. Pipe tube 1 centers and set aside to dry.

Prepare trims in advance

FOR TEN CURVED HEARTS on lower tier, tape patterns to curved surface. Tape wax paper smoothly over them and outline designs with tube 14. Dry, then attach flowers with dots of icing and trim with tube 349 leaves.

FOR TOP ORNAMENT, glue a filigree heart to plate. Cut 3″ squares of tulle and push centers into heart openings to form poufs. Attach flowers and pipe tube 349 leaves.

Prepare the tiers

First glue legs to underside of 16″ plate. Cut holes in centers of a 12″ and an 8″ cardboard cake circle (to receive column).

Bottom tier consists of a 12″ round layer plus a 12″ top bevel. Upper tier is an 8″ round layer plus 8″ top bevel. Fill layers, set on prepared cardboard bases and cover with marzipan, then rolled fondant. Cut hole in center of 12″ tier with a cake corer. Assemble tiers on 10″ and 16″ plates with column.

Divide bottom tier in tenths and mark on side 2½″ up from base. Divide upper tier in eighths and mark 2″ up from base. Marks will be your guides for fluted ruffles.

Decorate the cake

ON BOTTOM TIER, pipe tube 33 shells at base and trim with tube 104 ruffles. Drop string guidelines, then pipe fluted ruffles on side with tube 103, leaving 1″ between each curved ruffle. For an outstanding ruffle like this, hold the tube with wide end against tier side, narrow end straight out. Move your hand in a tight zigzag motion.

ON TOP TIER, trim is similar. Use tubes 21 and 104 for base border, 102 for side ruffle and 101s for bows at points of ruffles.

ATTACH FLOWERED HEARTS to bevel slant on bottom tier with dots of icing. Ring column with flowers and form clusters between scallops. Form a ring of flowers at top of upper tier and trim all flowers with tube 349 leaves. Set ornament in place. Sentimental is complete! Serve lower tier to 68 guests.

Rosy Dream

shown on page 111

See how pretty a petite cake can be! Trim the rosy tiers with pink impatiens blossoms—they're quickly made from gum paste.

ASSEMBLE ACCESSORIES: Flower garden cutter set; two 8″ round separator plates; four 5″ Corinthian pillars; Angel fountain; Petite top ornament.

Make the flowers

Follow the instructions in the booklet that comes with the cutter set. The impatiens is one of the fastest and easiest flowers to make in gum paste—and the results are charming. Form the finished flowers and leaves into clusters by twisting stems together and wrapping with floral tape.

Prepare the two-layer tiers

Bake, fill and ice the tiers—12″ x 4″ square and 8″ x 3″ round. Assemble on cake board with pillars and plates.

Mark the tiers with heart cookie cutters. Use a 2½″ cutter to pattern sides and top of bottom tier. Use a 2″ cutter to mark four evenly spaced hearts on side of upper tier.

Decorate the cake

ON BOTTOM TIER, pipe tube 22 shells around base, then frame with tube 14 zigzags on cake board. Between shells, pipe tube 14 stars. Edge separator plate with tube 6. Outline all hearts with tube 13 curved shells. Pipe a tube 16 reverse shell top border.

ON TOP TIER, pipe a tube 15 bottom shell border. Outline hearts with tube 13 curved shells. Pipe a tube 13 reverse shell top border.

ADD FLOWER TRIM. Push stems of clusters into tiers as pictured. Within hearts, attach leaves and flowers without stems, using royal icing. Secure angel to separator plate and trim with flowers. Trim ornament with flowers, then secure to cake top. Place Rosy Dream on the reception table and listen to the oohs and ahs! Serve lower tier to 72 guests.

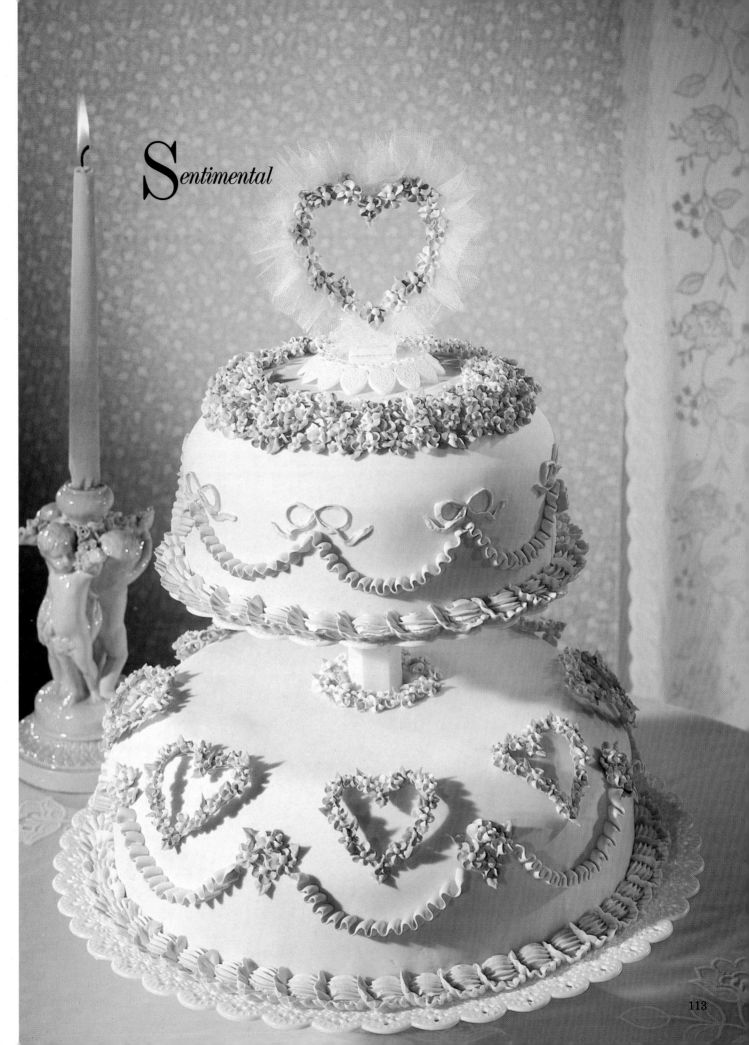

Sentimental

Bluebell

The prettiest way to give the bride "something blue" on her wedding day. Make the flowers in advance, then decorating the cake is quick and easy.

ASSEMBLE ACCESSORIES: one 8″ and one 10″ separator plate and eight twist legs (from Crystal clear set); top ornament.

Pipe the flowers

Use tube 66, a 1¼″ lily nail and royal icing. Press out three evenly spaced petals from center of well of nail, moving out to nail's edge. Add three more petals, one between each of first three. Pipe a tube 4 dot in center of flower and insert a few articial stamens.

Prepare the two-layer tiers

Bake, fill and ice the petal-shaped tiers—12″ x 4″, 9″ x 4″ and 6″ x 3″. Assemble with legs and plates on 15″ foil-covered cake board.

Decorate the cake

PIPE SHELL BORDERS at bottoms of all tiers. Use tube 17 for base tier, tube 16 for middle and top tiers. Pipe ruffly top borders on all tiers with tube 87 zigzags.

ADD FLOWER TRIM. Set ornament on cake top and add four clusters of bluebells, attaching with royal icing. Attach a flower to each indentation at base of tier. On two lower tiers, make cascades of bluebells. Pipe a mound of icing on top of tier, extending slightly over edge. Press in flowers. Trim all flowers with tube 67 leaves. Serve two lower tiers of this flowery centerpiece to 64 guests. Top tier will be frozen for the first anniversary.

114

Love's messenger

A petite wedding cake with surprising importance and charm. Golden roses are heaped on the lower tier.

ASSEMBLE ACCESSORIES: two 7″ separator plates; four 7″ Corinthian pillars; Cupid with arrow; Petite top ornament.

Pipe royal icing flowers

Pipe two-tone roses with tube 104. Do centers with yellow icing, outer petals with cream-color icing. Do rosebuds with same tube. Pipe wild roses with tube 101.

Prepare the two-layer tiers

Bake, fill and ice 10″ x 4″ and 6″ x 3″ round tiers. Assemble on cake board with pillars and plates. Divide 10″ tier into sixteenths and mark 1″ above base. Divide 6″ tier into sixteenths and mark 1″ above base.

Decorate the cake

ON BASE TIER, pipe a tube 22 bottom shell border. Over it, drop tube 15 string from mark to mark. Drop a second row of strings above this. Pipe a tube 20 reverse shell top border. Edge separator plate with tube 19.

ON TOP TIER, pipe a tube 19 bottom shell border. Pipe tube 14 scallops from mark to mark, then add tube 16 fleurs-de-lis and stars. Finish top edge with tube 19 reverse shells.

TRIM WITH FLOWERS. Set ornament on top tier and trim with flowers, attaching with royal icing. Set cupid on separator plate. Surround with flowers, forming sprays to drape over edge of lower tier. Secure a wild rose and two rosebuds to points of string drapes. Trim all flowers with tube 66 leaves. Lower tier of Love's Messenger will serve 48 guests. Freeze the top tier for the first anniversary celebration.

115

Lace Fan

A unique little masterpiece!
Tailored but very feminine borders
surround the tiers. The feature is a
lacy fan of lattice below top tier.

ASSEMBLE ACCESSORIES: 5½" plate,
5" pan and four legs from Mini-tier
set; Petite ornament; Flower spike.

Prepare trim and tiers
PIPE DROP FLOWERS in royal icing
with tubes 224 and 225. Mount two
dozen flowers on wire stems.

BAKE AND FILL the tiers—a 10" x 4"
two-layer square, single-layer 8"
and 5" rounds. Cover with rolled
fondant and assemble on cake
board. Transfer pattern to
middle tier.

Decorate the cake
PIPE A TUBE 1D BORDER on base tier,
a tube 2B border on middle tier.
Trim both with tube 2 scallops and
dots. (Don't be concerned if corners
on base tier are rough. Flowers will
cover them.)

SCALLOPED FAN DESIGN on middle
tier is over-piped. First outline with
tube 5, then build up with tubes 4, 3
and 3. Dry, then cover this
over-piping with tube 48. Drop tube
1 strings from scalloped edge to
inner circle. Finish with tube 1
beading. Insert flower spike in
center of tier, twist stems on wired
flowers and insert in spike.

ON TOP TIER, pipe a tube 4 bead
border, tube 2 scallops and dots.
Attach clusters of flowers to
corners of base tier and trim
ornament with flowers. Two lower
tiers of Lace Fan serve 65 guests.

Daisy Bower
Directions, page 118

Pipe flowers in advance

Use the fast Philippine method and royal icing to pipe the daisies. Direction are on page 12. Pipe tube 67 leaves on wire stems.

Make baskets and ornament

Roll out gum paste about ⅛" thick. Cut a strip about ⅞" x 6½", then mold over basket nail, dusted with cornstarch. Trim to fit. Dry 24 hours, then remove from nail. Pipe royal icing basketweave over basket, using tube 3 for vertical lines, tube 13 for horizontal strokes. Add tube 13 borders. Make handle by rolling a long gum paste cylinder and bending into an arch the width of a basket top and about 3" high. Secure a small piece of styrofoam in each basket with royal icing. Attach dried handle with icing. Arrange daisies.

Remove gates and fence from archway. Twine wires of flowers and leaves on arch, then glue angel fountain on base.

Prepare tiers, decorate cake

Glue legs to bottom of 16" plate and screw on column. Cut cardboard cake circles to sizes of tiers by tracing 6", 9" and 15" petal pans. Cut a hole in 9" and 15" circles to receive column. Bake two-layer petal-shaped tiers, 15" x 4", 9" x 4" and 6" x 3". Place on prepared cake circles, fill and ice. With cake corer, cut a hole in 15" tier. Assemble with plates and column.

ON BASE TIER, pipe tube 14 shells around center post. Press a 2" round cookie cutter to each side curve to guide piping. Pipe tube 16 bottom shell border. Pipe tube 14 fleurs-de-lis and stars. Frame with curves and scrolls. Pipe a tube 14 top shell border.

ON MIDDLE TIER, pipe a tube 15 bottom shell border. Drop tube 13 strings on each curve. Pipe stars, then add top shell border.

ON TOP TIER, pipe a tube 14 bottom shell border. Center a tube 13 fleur-de-lis topped with star on each curve. Add two "C" shapes beneath it and a star above it with same tube. Top border is tube 13 shells.

Clip stems off daisies to complete trim on ornament and base tier. Secure baskets to top of 15" tier. Serve two lower tiers of Daisy Bower to 82 guests.

Daisy Bower

shown on page 117

An outstanding cake to show off your decorating skills. Dainty gum paste baskets are filled with daisies—more daisies flower on the arched ornament.

ASSEMBLE ACCESSORIES: Australian basket nails; Angel fountain; Picket archway; 16" and 10" plates, four glue-on legs and a 6½" column (from Tall tier stand); Cake corer.

Golden Dawn

Airy daisies and yellow wild roses trim this sunshiny petite cake.

ASSEMBLE ACCESSORIES: Harvest cherub separator set, three Mediterranean cupids; top plate from Heart ornament base; Petite ornament.

Make flowers in advance

Use royal icing and tube 103 for daisies. Add tube 5 centers. Pipe wild roses with tube 103. Dry all flowers within curves.

Prepare the two-layer tiers

Bake and fill the 14" x 4" and 8" x 3" tiers. Cover with rolled fondant. Assemble on cake board with separator set. Divide side of 14" tier in twelfths and mark 2" up from base and at top edge. Divide side of 8" tier in twelfths and mark ¾" up from bottom and at top edge.

DECORATE BASE TIER Make a star bottom border with tube 17 and trim with tube 3 loops. Drop string guidelines from lower marks on tier side and pipe tube 5 circular motion garlands. Top with double tube 3 strings and "Italian" bows. On top edge of tier, drop string guidelines from mark to mark. Pipe circular motion tube 16 garlands, then trim with double tube 3 strings. Mark shallow scallops on the tier top to connect each garland, then fill in from scallops to separator plate with tube 1 cornelli. Edge plate with tube 4 bulbs and outline scallops with same tube.

ON TOP TIER, do bottom "hanging" border when cake is on the reception table. From top edge of tier, drop string guidelines for garlands. With tube 4, connect garlands on top of the tier in scallops. Fill in space between scallops and guidelines with tube 1 cornelli. Pipe garlands and scallops with tube 3 zigzags.

Attach ornaments within pillars and on top of cake. Circle the seated cherubs with wild roses, then trim ornaments and tiers with flowers.

On the reception table, pipe bottom border on 8" tier. Drop guidelines, then pipe zigzag tube 4 garlands. Trim with tube 3 string and flowers. Lower tier serves 92.

Golden Dawn

Edwardian Rose

A white dove, symbol of love and peace, floats on a richly scrolled cake of unusual construction.

Do trims in advance

MAKE BLUE PLAQUE from pattern and rolled gum paste. When dry, edge with tube 2 bulbs. Figure pipe dove of royal icing directly on a 10″ curved form covered with wax paper. Only tube 2 is used. First build up body with heavy pressure. Pull out head, piping tiny beak. Pipe two heavy lines for tops of wings, then quickly pipe wing feathers in three layers, starting with outer edges. Pipe fan-shaped tail, and add blue dot for eye. Dry.

MAKE ROYAL ICING FLOWERS. Pipe roses, tiny to large, using tubes 101s, 101, 102, 103, and 104. Pipe several sizes of daisies with tube 102 petals. Dry daisies on curved surface. Pipe spikes on backs of several larger roses.

Prepare tiers, decorate cake

Bake, fill and ice two 9″ oval layers and two 9″ x 13″ layers. Assemble on ruffle-trimmed cake board. Transfer patterns to tiers, or use your own scroll designs.

PIPE CURVES AND FLOWERS on tier sides with tube 5, varying pressure. Pipe swirls on top of base tier, then pipe tube 5 bulbs for all borders. Use lighter pressure as you go up.

ATTACH DOVE to plaque with mounds of royal icing. Set plaque on cake, supporting with sugar cubes and mounds of icing. Trim plaque and top of cake with smallest flowers, adding tube 65 leaves. Then arrange a spray of flowers and tube 67 leaves to cascade down cake. Insert spiked flowers in side of lower tier. Serve lower tier of this elegant confection to 54 guests.

Baroque Heart

A stunning cake in the old world style. Baroque gum paste designs give it flair.

ASSEMBLE ACCESSORIES: two 6" heart separator plates; three 3" Grecian pillars; Baroque gum paste mold set.

Make trims in advance

MAKE EIGHT ROYAL CREST gum paste designs and three angelica designs using baroque molds. Follow directions that come with the molds. Dry the angelicas on largest curved form. Dry royal crests on side of a 12" heart pan covered with wax paper. When designs are dry, pipe two "spikes" with royal icing and tube 6 on back of each royal crest. On back of two angelica designs, pipe a spike at base of wings. On one angelica design, pipe two spikes extending from lower edge of wings.

PIPE ROSES AND BUDS, with tubes 102 and 103. When dry, mount most on wire stems. Pipe tube 65 leaves on wire. Make sprays of wired flowers and leaves.

Prepare tiers, decorate cake

BAKE TIERS—a two-layer 12" heart and single-layer 9" and 6" hearts. Fill and ice and assemble on cake board with pillars and plates. Divide each half of 12" tier into fourths and mark 1½" up from base. Divide each half of 9" tier into sevenths and mark near top edge.

ON BASE TIER, pipe a tube 16 fleur-de-lis at each mark, then pipe a shell border around bottom. Pipe a shell border at top of tier, extending shells into plume design above each fleur-de-lis.

ON MIDDLE TIER, use tube 16 to pipe shell-and-plume base border. Use marks as guides for plumes. Edge separator plate with scallops. Pipe tube 14 shell-and-plume border on top tier.

PUSH IN ROYAL CREST designs on base tier on mounds of icing. Arrange flowers between pillars. Push in angelica designs, supporting with mounds of icing. Arrange flowers around angelicas. Serve two lower tiers of Baroque Heart to 62 guests.

CHAPTER SIX

Delightful cakes in the Australian style

A PERFECT STYLE for wedding cakes! The unmistakeable cakes done in the Australian style are perfectly proportioned, delicately tinted and adorned with the daintiest of details. The tiers are covered in rolled fondant to give a satiny background for the trims— fragile see-through curtaining, precise embroidery and fine lace. The gum paste flowers are equally dainty and delicate.

In the Australian style, no detail is ever bold or flamboyant. Everything is scaled to a petite, fine proportion. The result is a cake as pretty as a bridal gown.

TO WORK IN THIS STYLE, the decorator needs a skilled, controlled hand to pipe with the smallest of round tubes, and to gracefully furl the petals of the flowers. While every Australian method cake will show the hallmarks of the style, each will be unique. Each decorator develops her own style of freehand embroidery and piping. Even the flower arrangements will have a personality that reflects the decorator's taste and skill.

Rose Blush

THE BEAUTIFUL CAKE at left was decorated by Marie Grainger, a highly skilled and innovative Australian decorator. Mrs. Grainger has taught and demonstrated her techniques in Europe, America and many foreign countries, in addition to her native country. Rose Blush displays some of her time-saving techniques as well as her artistic touch with gum paste flowers.

Mrs. Grainger's recipes are on page 127. Use egg white royal icing for all trims.

Do trims in advance

Marie Grainger pipes the fragile lace pieces freehand—but we are showing her pattern in the Appendix. Use tube 000.

THE GUM PASTE FLOWERS are shown and described on the next pages. The gum paste bells are molded over bell molds, then the edges are given a lacy edge with a cutter. When dry, a royal icing design is piped on.

Prepare the tiers

In the Australian method, each tier is set on its own cake board. The tiers are simply stacked on pillars so they are easy to remove for serving.

Australian wedding cakes are made of fruitcake, covered first with marzipan, then rolled fondant. Marie Grainger brushes the cake with syrup rather than apricot glaze. She uses the syrup to brush the marzipan before smoothing on the fondant, too. Base tier in Rose Blush is 11" square x 2¾", middle tier 8½" x 2½", top tier 6" x 2¼". Set each covered tier on its foil-covered cake board.

For perfect harmony, the 3" Grecian pillars are sprayed to match the ivory color of the cake. Set four of them in position on the base tier. Push a ¼" dowel rod through the opening in each pillar until it touches the cake board below, then clip off level with the top of the pillar. The pillars on the middle tier are attached in the same fashion.

Decorate the cake

First transfer the patterns to the tiers. Attach narrow ribbon with a thin line of icing. All trim is done in royal icing.

PIPE THE TRIM. Pipe a tube 4 line of icing all around the base of each tier. Now pipe the extension to hold the curtaining, with three lines of tube 4. These quick finishes are time-savers originated by Mrs. Grainger. Starting ⅛" below ribbon, pipe the curtaining with tube 000. Adding a very small amount of light corn syrup to the royal icing will help you in piping perfectly straight, even lines.

PIPE THE EMBROIDERY on all three tiers with tube 000, freehand.

ADD THE LACE PIECES. Mrs. Grainger does this by piping a tube 1 line, about 6" long at the top of the curtaining. A lace piece is quickly set in place, then two dots are piped, a second lace piece, two more dots. Continue until you have attached lace to the length of the line, then pipe another line and add lace and dots in the same way. At the bottom of the curtaining, pipe a tube 000 line and top with dots, first in triplets, then singly.

A LITTLE BIRD, symbol of happiness, rests near the flower spray on the top tier. The wings and tail are piped separately with tube 000— the body figure piped. Wings and tail are inserted into the still-wet body. Finished bird is only ½" long!

ARRANGE THE FLOWER SPRAYS on the tiers and the beautiful cake is complete. Australian servings are sample-sized—1" x 1" x 2". Cutting the cake in the American way into pieces two layers by 1" wide x 2" deep will give you 82 servings from the two lower tiers.

Gum paste flowers the new Australian way

MARIE GRAINGER uses flower trim on her Australian cakes in a casual, natural way that shows them off at their best. Her flowers are small and never overpower the fine proportion and dainty details of the cake itself. Each is perfectly formed with petals gracefully furled. The flowers at right are shown a little larger than actual size to bring out their detail. With the exception of the rose, they are not given botanical names—just titles.

TOOLS USED to make the flowers are simple. Most flowers and leaves are cut with special cutters of Mrs. Grainger's design. Wire stems for small flowers are as fine as threads. Heavier flowers, like the rose, are mounted on stiffer, heavier wires. Her gum paste recipe is on page 127. It is tinted in the most delicate hues with liquid food color. Often the flowers are fashioned from untinted gum paste. Then the petals are delicately brushed with powdered non-toxic chalk, applied with an artist's brush. Satin ribbons add to the dainty effect of an arrangement. Use ⅛″ wide ribbon, or cut wider ribbon to that width.

Making the rose

MODEL A BALL from gum paste, about ½″ in diameter. Insert a hooked florists' wire, then shape the ball into a pointed cone. Allow to dry 48 hours, so make these bases for the rose ahead of time.

TINT A LITTLE GUM PASTE a delicate pink and roll out very thin. Cut a petal with the smallest rose cutter, thin one side by pressing with your fingers. Wrap around the base in a sideways position, first brushing on a little water to secure. Cut three more small petals. Thin and furl the edges, right side back, left side forward. Apply a little water and wrap around base.

FOR NEXT FOUR PETALS, work the pink gum paste with an equal amount of white gum paste until evenly tinted. Roll out as thin as possible and cut four petals with the medium rose cutter. Thin and furl edges with your fingers and apply to the base with water.

FOR NEXT FIVE PETALS, lighten the gum paste again by kneading in an equal amount of untinted gum paste. Roll out slightly thicker than for the other petals and cut with the largest rose cutter. Furl the rounded edges and just lay them on the rose, applying no pressure. Dry the flower overnight in cornstarch.

Making the lily

FORM A BALL of gum paste about ⅜″ in diameter. Press all around with your fingers to make a hat shape, crown thick and rounded, edges thin. Cut out with the largest lily cutter. The thickness at the center gives strength to the flower.

SHAPE WITH YOUR FINGERS into a deep-throated flower, thinning and furling the five petals.

BIND SEVEN OR EIGHT artificial stamens together with thin florists' wire. Insert the end of the wire through the center of the flower. Press all around the base of the flower to secure. Make smaller lilies with the medium lily cutter.

Making the blossom

The technique is similar to that of the lily. Start with a ¼″ ball. Thin edges to a hat shape, about as big as a nickel. Cut with the smallest lily cutter. Again, the center will be thick, edges very thin.

TO CUP THE PETALS, press with the rounded end of a stick, as you hold the flower very lightly with three fingers. Bind five artificial stamens, about ½″ long, with fine wire. Insert wire through center of flower and press base of flower around it.

TO MAKE A BUD, form a tiny ball of gum paste, insert hooked wire and shape into a cone. Score in five places with an artist's knife.

BLUSH THE BLOSSOM and bud very delicately with powdered, non-toxic chalk. Twist stems together and dry overnight. Make other flowers by using the same method, but using different cutters.

Looping the ribbons

Use satin ribbons ⅛″ wide, or cut wider ribbon to ⅛″ width. Arrange in loops, then bind with fine wire. Add the ribbon loops to flower arrangements.

Making lily of the valley

Roll out a little gum paste about 1/16″ thick. Cut flower shapes with a tiny six-petaled cutter. Hold shape on tips of thumb and two fingers and press all around with the rounded end of a stick to cup and thin the flower. Make a tiny hook on the end of a length of fine florists' wire. Pull the wire through the flower, slightly off center. For bud, model a tiny ball of gum paste. Pull a hooked wire through it, then shape the ball with your fingers.

Making leaves

Roll gum paste, tinted the palest green, very thin. Cut the leaf, then vein in a leaf mold. Press edges to thin, then pinch base with your fingers to furl. Lay on cornstarch to dry, then brush with powdered non-toxic chalk.

To reproduce these flowers, you may use the small and large violet leaf and orchid cutters for roses, the violet and briar rose cutters for lilies and blossoms. All are from the Flower garden set. For lily of the valley, use the metal forget-me-not cutter. Your flowers will be a little larger.

MAKING THE ROSE

MAKING LILIES

MAKING BLOSSOMS

LOOPING RIBBONS

MAKING LEAVES

MAKING LILY OF THE VALLEY

Fantasy

DELICATE CLUSTERS of pale mauve and pink blossoms garland a graceful oval cake. This creation by Marie Grainger shows the same innovative techniques as Rose Blush on page 122—yet the cake retains the classic Australian style.

Pipe lace pieces in advance
Use egg white royal icing and tube 000. While these pieces were done freehand, you will find a pattern in the Appendix. Mrs. Grainger shares a quick technique for freehand piping of lace—pipe them directly on a cookie sheet with a non-stick surface. The dried lace slides off the pan easily.

Cover the tiers
Lower tier is a 12″ x 9″ x 3½″ oval, top oval tier is 8″ x 5″ x 3″ high. If you do not have oval pans in these measurements, modify the design by using 12″ and 8″ round pans. Cover the fruit cake tiers first with marzipan, then with rolled fondant. Use the method shown on page 129. Use either the Marie Grainger recipes, next page, or the Wilton recipes, pages 163 and 164. Note that both tiers rest on foil-covered cake boards. The one below the base tier is 3″ larger all around than the tier.

ATTACH THE 3″ PILLARS by setting them in position on the lower tier, then pushing ¼″ dowel rods through the pillar openings until they rest on the cake board. Clip off dowels even with tops of pillars.

Make the flowers
Use the methods shown on page 125 for the gum paste flowers. Do the

126

rosebuds in palest pink. The other blossoms are made of white gum paste, delicately brushed with powdered non-toxic chalk. Form little clusters of flowers and loops of narrow satin ribbon.

Decorate the cake

All trim is done in egg white royal icing.

ATTACH RIBBON by piping a thin line of icing around lower tier, 2½″ up from base. Press ribbon onto the line of icing. Do the same on the upper tier, piping the line 2″ up from base of tier.

MARK THE TIERS to guide piping. The curtaining starts 1¼″ above the cake boards on both tiers. Top points of scallops are ⅜″ above cake boards. There are 72 scalloped extensions on lower tier, 50 on· upper tier.

PIPE THE EMBROIDERY freehand with tube 000. Note the tiny pink dot flowers and scattering of stylized green leaves. The rest of the embroidery is white.

AT BASE OF BOTH TIERS, pipe a tube 4 line of icing. Now pipe the scalloped extension work with three lines of tube 4. Page 132 shows method. Follow the marks to guide piping.

Now drop the tube 000 lines of curtaining. Drop two tiny curves of string from lower points of each scallop. Top with spaced dots.

ATTACH LACE PIECES by piping a tube 1 line about 6″ long just above curtaining on lower tier. Hold lace pieces on line to attach, leaving a space between each. When you have attached lace to the length of the line, pipe another 6″ line and attach lace. Continue until tier is circled. Attach lace to upper tier the same way, adding two tube 1 dots between each.

ARRANGE FLOWER CLUSTERS in a garland around lower tier. Set ornament* on cake top, hang bells and attach flower sprays at base and top. Fantasy is exquisite! Serve both tiers to 98 guests.

Recipes for Marie Grainger's Australian cakes

Gum paste

3 teaspoons unflavored gelatin
3 tablespoons water
1 teaspoon lemon juice
1 tablespoon solid white vegetable shortening
1 tablespoon light corn syrup
1 pound, 2 ounces sifted confectioners' sugar

Soak gelatin in the water and lemon juice for 30 minutes in an enamel saucepan. Place the shortening and corn syrup on top of water and gelatin. Melt on the lowest heat, then knead in sugar. Store in an airtight plastic container in the refrigerator for weeks. Pat top of gum paste with water before sealing.

Syrup

For brushing the cake before putting on marzipan and for brushing the marzipan before smoothing on fondant.

1 cup granulated sugar
½ cup water
¾ cup light corn syrup

Place all ingredients in a saucepan, bring to a boil and simmer gently for ten to fifteen minutes. Store tightly sealed in the refrigerator for months.

Marzipan

1 pound confectioners' sugar (approximate)

4 ounces almond paste
2 egg yolks
2 tablespoons sherry
2 tablespoons light corn syrup
¼ cup lemon juice

Place the sugar and almond paste in a large bowl, add the egg yolks and sherry, corn syrup and lemon juice. Knead until mixture is pliable and resembles pie dough, adding extra sugar if necessary.

Fruit cake

You will need 2¼ recipes for the cake on page 122

1 pound raisins
1 pound currants
1 pound sultanas
6 ounces candied cherries, chopped
6 ounces mixed candied peel, chopped
4 ounces dried apricots, chopped
¾ cup sherry
1 pound butter
1 pound brown sugar
10 eggs
1 pound, 4 ounces flour, sifted
1 teaspoon ginger
1 teaspoon mixed spice
1 teaspoon nutmeg
1 teaspoon lemon flavoring
1 teaspoon almond flavoring
1 teaspoon vanilla
1 heaping tablespoon dark corn syrup
1 tablespoon vinegar
2 tablespoons rum

Preheat oven to 350°F. Place all fruit in a bowl and pour sherry over it. Allow to soak while you proceed with recipe. Cream butter and sugar, add eggs, one at a time, with a little of the sifted flour. Add all spices and flavorings, corn syrup, vinegar and rum. Stir in soaked fruit.

Add remaining flour. Spoon into well-greased pans.

Place in 350°F oven for one hour. Lower heat to 250°F for remainder of baking time—approximately six hours.

Rolled fondant

Two recipes are needed for the cake on page 122.

2 pounds sifted confectioners' sugar (approximate)
4 tablespoons Color Flow mix
½ cup water
6 tablespoons light corn syrup

Place confectioners' sugar into large bowl, add Color Flow mix and blend together. Add water and corn syrup and mix well. When fondant becomes too stiff to mix, remove from bowl to smooth surface and knead, adding extra sugar as necessary.

The clear plastic ornament was made by Mr. John Grainger.

A heart-shaped cake in the classic Australian style

This dainty little cake was designed as a centerpiece for a shower or announcement party, but it's so beautiful it could be the bridal cake itself for an intimate wedding.

By studying the steps for its decoration you will learn just how to create a cake in the classic Australian method. The next three pages will show you how to cover a cake with rolled fondant, pipe extensions, do curtaining and embroidery, then add the final touch of gum paste flowers.

Prepare the cake

Bake two layers of fruit cake in 9" heart pans. Each layer should be 1½" high. Use the recipe on page 164, or your own favorite. Fill the layers with apricot jam, then follow the pictured steps shown below to cover the cake with rolled fondant. With a little practice you'll be able to cover the cake in ten or fifteen minutes.

Attach a cardboard cake circle the same size and shape to bottom of cake with a few strokes of royal icing. Make a recipe of marzipan. Fill any holes and crevices with small pieces of marzipan. Brush cake top and sides with apricot glaze. Dust work surface with confectioners' sugar, then roll out marzipan to a ⅜" thick circle large enough to cover the entire cake surface. Fold the marzipan over the rolling pin, place on edge of the cake and unroll marzipan onto the cake.

Gently press marzipan into place around cake and smooth with palms of hands. Marzipan has no stretch and sometimes, when covering a cake, cracks will appear. If this happens, pinch the crack together and rub it gently with palm of hand until there is a smooth surface.

Cut off excess marzipan at base with a sharp knife. Let harden for at least twelve hours. This will prevent the oil from the marzipan from seeping through the fondant covering. Now the cake with its seamless covering is ready to be covered with rolled fondant.

Brush marzipan covering with apricot glaze. Coat work surface with a thin layer of nonstick pan release and dust with cornstarch. Roll fondant out to a ¼" thick circle large enough to cover entire cake. Fold the fondant over the rolling pin, place on end of cake and unroll. Smooth fondant into place.

Cut off excess fondant around base. Then smooth again with hands and trim excess fondant off again, so the bottom edge is perfectly even. As you smooth the fondant, it will become slightly glossy. Transfer cake to cake board or serving plate.

Now the cake is ready to be decorated. The layers of marzipan and rolled fondant seal in the moisture of the fruit cake and give a perfectly smooth surface on which to decorate.

Please turn the page

Do trims in advance

PIPE LACE PIECES, using pattern in the Appendix and egg white royal icing. Tape patterns to a stiff surface, tape wax paper over them. Pipe with tube 1s.

MAKE GUM PASTE FLOWERS. Use the Flower Garden cutter set and directions on the next page. Before making the roses and stephanotis, read the general information in the booklet that comes with the cutters.

After the flowers have dried, twist stems together and wrap with floral tape. Cut several 3″ squares of fine tulle and bunch at the centers with fine wire. Add to the flower cluster and tie with a ribbon bow.

Mark the cake

First attach the covered cake to a foil-covered cake board cut 1½″ larger than the cake all around. Using cake pan as guide, make a 6″ heart pattern and mark a 5″ heart within it. Transfer to cake top, then write message with tube 1s and a mixture of half royal icing, half piping gel. Transfer pattern for curtaining to cake sides, lowest point about ⅜″ above base. Mark pattern on cake at point of heart first, then on sides, skipping one space to allow room for ribbon. Curtaining will not meet at back of heart at indentation. Attach ribbon from inner heart to base of cake with dots of icing.

Decorate the cake

Use egg white royal icing for all piping. Make sure it is lump-free by sieving the sugar three times before mixing the icing. Pipe a tube 4 bulb border at base of cake.

FILL THE MARKED HEART with tube 000 cornelli lace, then edge heart with a "snail's trail" (bulb border) and tiny scallops. Edge ribbon with beading. Pipe the embroidery at top edge and sides of cake freehand with the same tube.

PIPE EXTENSION AND CURTAINING. Pipe scalloped extension to support curtaining with tube 1. First pipe a line the full width of the base of each triangle, then a second, shorter line on top and in the center of it. Repeat four more times, making a total of six lines, each line shorter than the one preceding it. After piping two lines, pause to let the icing dry. Finally pipe a finishing line around each little "shelf". Brush surface with thinned icing to smooth. Dry.

Pipe the fragile curtaining with tube 000. Drop strings from top of triangles to extensions, keeping spaces perfectly even. Dry thoroughly, then edge with "snail's trails" and tiny dropped strings.

ATTACH LACE PIECES to heart. Pipe a few dots of icing to base of a lace piece, then hold to cake an instant until set. Keep pieces at a uniform angle. Add a ribbon bow at base, and set bouquet on cake top. The curtaining does not meet at back of cake where heart indents, so place second gum paste rose there. Serve wedding cake-size pieces to 28.

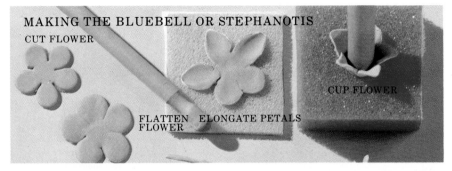

MAKING THE BLUEBELL OR STEPHANOTIS

CUT FLOWER

FLATTEN FLOWER ELONGATE PETALS

CUP FLOWER

Make five stephanotis

The form of this five-petaled flower is the same as the bluebell, so we show the quick blue bell steps.

CUT ONE-PIECE FLOWER with the violet cutter from thinly rolled untinted gum paste. Flatten by lightly rolling with rolling pin.

LAY FLOWER ON FOAM TOWELING. Elongate petals by laying the rounded end of a stick on center of each petal. Pull out the stick toward tip of petal, pressing lightly.

CUP FLOWER by laying it on a soft foam sponge. Press rounded end of a stick in the center. Cut a tiny hole in center of flower and pull an artificial stamen through it. Wrap stem of stamen with floral tape and dry upside down on a cotton ball. When dry, pipe a ball of yellow icing over the stamen.

Make two roses

MAKE THE BUD FIRST. Tint a small amount of gum paste. Model a little cone, ½" high. Bend the end of a length of florists' wire into a tiny hook. Insert it into the cone. Roll out a little gum paste as thin as possible and cut 2 petals with the small rose cutter. Use the rolling pin to roll the petals into two ovals. Overlap the petals, place on foam toweling and furl them by rolling edges with a stick. Wrap around cone, securing with egg white.

ADD MORE PETALS. Cut six petals with the medium rose cutter. Cut an arc from each with the same cutter, to make semi-petals. Furl semi-petals by placing on foam toweling and rolling outer edges with a stick. Brush inner edges with egg white and wrap around bud. Continue with remaining semi-petals. For a small rose, furl the petals outward, add calyx and stick into styrofoam to dry.

FOR A FULL-BLOWN, many-petaled rose, add six more petals. Cut them with the medium rose cutter. Roll into ovals with the rolling pin. Make a pleat in the long side of a petal, lay on foam toweling and roll edge with a stick. Brush base of small rose with egg white and wrap petal around it, pleat toward wire. Furl edge of petal outward. Continue with other five petals.

ADD CALYX. Cut with the calyx cutter from thinly rolled green gum paste. Place on foam toweling and press from tips to center with the round end of a stick. Make a tiny hole in center of calyx, brush center with egg white and slide over stem of rose, pressing to base. Wrap stem with floral tape and stick into styrofoam to dry.

MAKING THE LEAVES

Make the leaves

CUT LEAVES from green-tinted gum paste, thinly rolled, with the small rose leaf cutter. Press into leaf mold to vein. Dip the end of a length of florists' wire into egg white and attach to back. Dry.

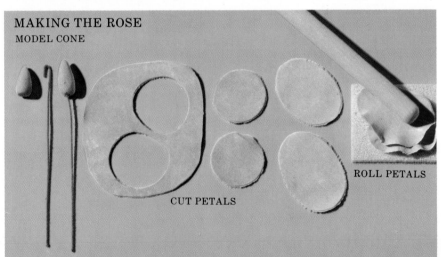

MAKING THE ROSE
MODEL CONE

CUT PETALS

ROLL PETALS

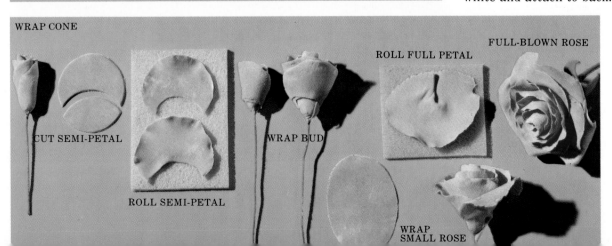

WRAP CONE

ROLL FULL PETAL

FULL-BLOWN ROSE

CUT SEMI-PETAL

WRAP BUD

ROLL SEMI-PETAL

WRAP SMALL ROSE

Australian Rose

This simple but very appealing little cake is a good one to begin with, if you are new to the Australian method of decorating.

Make trims in advance

MAKE THREE ROSES and four or five leaves from gum paste, following the directions on page 130. Note that the centers of the roses are tinted more deeply than the other petals.

MAKE FORGET-ME-NOTS in blue-tinted gum paste. Roll out and cut eighteen or twenty flowers with the tiny metal forget-me-not cutter. Cut off tips on one side of artificial stamens. Form a tiny (less than ¼") gum paste ball. Pass cut end of stamen through flower shape, then through ball. Taper ball around stamen stem. With your fingers, shape some flowers open, close others to bud shape. Dry, then make six sprays by taping three flowers and buds to a length of fine florists' wire. Wrap wire with floral tape.

MAKE TULLE HANDKERCHIEFS. Cut three 4" squares of fine tulle, lay on wax paper, and pipe scalloped borders with royal icing and tube 1. Pick up handkerchief in center, letting it fall in natural folds, and bind center with fine wire.

ARRANGE BOUQUET. Twist stems of roses, leaves and forget-me-not sprays together. Add handkerchiefs. Wrap with floral tape.

PIPE LACE PIECES. Tape patterns to a stiff surface and tape wax paper smoothly over them. Pipe with tube 1s and egg white royal icing. You will need 60, but make extras.

Prepare the cake

Bake an 8"x 3 round fruit cake. Cover the cake with marzipan, then rolled fondant just as shown on page 129. Place on foil-covered cake board.

MAKE A SIX-POINTED STAR pattern. Fold a 12" circle of paper into sixths, fan fashion. Snip a point at open end. Transfer to cake, marking with a pin.

Decorate the cake

Pipe a tube 4 bulb border at base. Outline marked star pattern with tiny tube 1s scallops. Pipe freehand flower and leaf designs with the same tube.

Set bouquet on top of cake, securing on a mound of royal icing. Now add the lace pieces. Just outside scallops, pipe a short line with tube 1. Set in lace piece, holding an instant until set. Continue until entire star is outlined with lace. Australian Rose serves 30 wedding guests.

Australian lace

An exquisite cake for an intimate wedding reception. The flounced curtaining, delicate embroidery and satin ribbons are all snow white—the only touches of color are the pale gold centers of the white roses and the blue of the bluebells.

Make trims in advance

THE GUM PASTE ROSES, bluebells and leaves are fashioned just as shown on page 131. Artificial pearl-tipped stamens center the bluebells.

MAKE THREE HANDKERCHIEFS of fine tulle, just as described above for Australian Rose. Twist stems of flowers, leaves and handkerchiefs into a bouquet, wrap with floral tape and tie with a ribbon bow.

Prepare the cake

Bake an 8" x 3" square fruit cake and cover with marzipan, then rolled fondant as shown on page 129. Set cake on a 14" foil-covered cake board.

Decorate the cake

Use egg white royal icing for all.

MAKE PATTERN for extension work and curtaining first. Measure circumference of cake with a 1" strip of paper, fold into 20 divisions and make pattern for scallops. Mark scallops very accurately on side of cake with tiny pin holes. Lower points of scallops are ⅜" above cake board.

Mark diagonal line across corners of cake for ribbon. Pipe a thin line of icing on marks, then attach ¼" wide ribbon. Pipe freehand dot flowers, leaves and beading on ribbon. Pipe a tube 4 bulb border around base of cake.

PIPE EXTENSION WORK. Drop a tube 2 string of royal icing along marked scallop and over-pipe four times, letting each line dry before piping another one. Position each line along outer edge of line beneath it to give the extension work an outward slant. When dry, brush with thinned royal icing. Dry.

MAKE CURTAINING. Pipe tube 1s strings from pin holes to extension work. To keep lines straight, pipe those at points of scallops first, then one directly in center. Divide the space on either side of center with a line and keep dividing open spaces until the scallop is covered with strings. Repeat around the cake. Pipe tube 1s beading along lower edge of extension work, then drop tiny string loops from it. Pipe tiny scallops along top of curtaining with tube 1s. Add dot flowers and leaves.

Attach bouquet on a mound of icing. Attach four tiny bows at lower points of ribbon. Serve Australian Lace to 32.

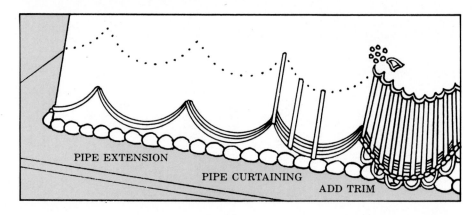

PIPE EXTENSION   PIPE CURTAINING   ADD TRIM

Australian Rose

Australian lace

CHAPTER SEVEN

Cakes for Wedding Anniversaries

NEXT TO THE WEDDING CAKE, an anniversary cake has the most sentimental appeal. These cakes bring back memories of the glorious wedding day, and are symbols that mark the years of married love.

In this chapter you'll find cakes that celebrate anniversaries from the first to the fiftieth. Those for a rather new marriage are fun and frivolous. Cakes for the twentieth to the fiftieth anniversary are more imposing, and are designed for big celebrations.

MANY OF THESE CAKES can be adapted for a bridal cake by just changing the color and trim. So browse through this chapter. You'll find lots of ideas for party cakes and wedding cakes, as well as cakes for wedding anniversaries.

A rosy cake for the 25th

25 blazing candles mark the years. The decorating is simple and quick, the effect is spectacular! The heart is the decorating motif, the flowers are arrangements of silk roses.

Assemble your accessories

Two 14" round separator plates
Four 7" Corinthian pillars
Anniversary ornament
Heart bowl
24 Stairsteps, inserts and candle holders
24 candles and one tall taper
Silk flowers
Silver artificial leaves

Prepare the two-layer tiers

BAKE, FILL AND ICE 16" x 4", 12" x 4" and 8" x 4" tiers. Assemble with plates and pillars. Mark center front and center back of all tiers midway on sides. Lightly press a 2½" heart cookie cutter to front and back of base tier. Press a 2" cutter to front and back of middle tier.

Decorate the cake

ON BASE TIER, outline marked heart with tube 16 curves. Pipe names with tube 1. Do the same on back of cake. Pipe a tube 199 bottom shell border, then trim with tube 103 ruffles. On top of tier, pipe a tube 17 reverse shell border, then outline separator plate with tube 16.

ON MIDDLE TIER, pipe marked heart and scrolls with tube 16. Pipe a tube 32 bottom shell border. Use tube 16 for reverse shells at top edge. Pipe heart and scrolls at center back.

ON TOP TIER, pipe three shell motion hearts at front and back with tube 16. Add curved shells and scrolls with same tube. Pipe a tube 17 shell border at bottom, reverse shell border at top.

Put it all together

FILL BOWL with a block of styrofoam. Insert taper, then ring with silk flowers. Add silver leaves and a ribbon. Trim ornament with flowers and leaves.

ATTACH FOUR STAIRSTEPS to side of base tier securing with inserts. Measuring carefully from center front, attach four stairsteps to other side of tier. Do the same with two upper tiers. Trim side of each stair with a tube 16 royal icing heart. Insert candles in holders and fit into stair. Set ornament within pillars and bowl of flowers on cake top.

At serving time, light all the candles for a thrilling effect. Serve two lower tiers to 186 guests. Present the top tier to the anniversary couple.

An airy masterpiece
for the 25th anniversary

Delicate see-through curves give dimension and a play of light and shadow to this important cake for an important occasion—the 25th wedding anniversary.

Make the baroque gum paste designs well ahead of time, then decorating the cake will be very quick and easy.

ASSEMBLE YOUR ACCESSORIES
Baroque gum paste mold set
Four twist legs from Crystal clear set
10" plate from Crystal clear set
Silver anniversary couple
Flower spike

Make gum paste trim ahead

Use the mantle design for these baroque curves. Read the instructions that come with the set, make a recipe of gum paste (page 164), tint it and you're ready to mold.

Here are the designs you'll need:
Four designs dried on 6" curved surface to surround the anniversary couple
Six designs dried on 8" curve for 8" tier and to set between tiers
Six designs dried on 12" curved surface for base tier. On four of these (as shown on front of cake) trim off the curves on one side while still wet.

When designs are completely dry, pipe royal icing spikes to attach them to the cake. Pipe spikes on bases of designs that stand upright, on backs of designs that lie against the sides of the base and top tiers.

Pipe drop flowers

Make drop flowers in royal icing with tubes 131,33 and 225. Add tube 2 centers and dry. Mount some flowers on wire stems, twist stems together and wrap with floral tape for bouquet between tiers.

Prepare tiers and decorate

BAKE TIERS—a 16" base bevel, 12" x 4" and 8" x 3" round. Also bake a small cake, 2" deep, and cut into a 3" circle as base for couple. Ice with buttercream. Set all tiers on cardboard cake circles, same size, and assemble with plate and legs. (Legs rest on cake circle below 12" tier.)

INSERT FLOWER SPIKE in center of 12" tier and set in bouquet. Pipe four pairs of tube 5 hearts on side of 3" circle cake. Place on top tier. Pipe tube 5 bulb borders at bases of all tiers.

ATTACH ALL GUM PASTE designs to cake, pressing in spikes and using mounds of icing for support. Pipe tube 5 hearts within designs. Do names with tube 1. Now trim cake with garlands of flowers, attaching with dots of icing. Set couple on cake top. Serves about 128 wedding cake-size slices (cut bevel tier in 30 pieces).

Cherub musicians pose on a lacy stairway to serenade the anniversary couple. This imposing centerpiece is very quickly decorated—jewel-like candy hearts and red silk roses carry out the ruby theme of the 40th anniversary.

ASSEMBLE YOUR ACCESSORIES

Filigree stairway set

Six Musical trio cherubs

4" Filigree heart and top plate from small Heart base (for ornament)

Top plate from large Heart base (for bouquet)

Two 10" and two 13" Hexagon separator plates

Twelve 5" Corinthian pillars

Bridal couple figures

Hard candy heart mold

Silk flowers

Do trims in advance

Mold candy hearts, using recipe on page 164. Cover tightly with plastic wrap until ready to use.

MAKE ORNAMENT. Glue the filigree heart to small top plate, then glue a cherub musician in front of heart. For bouquet within pillars, glue a small block of styrofoam to larger top plate. Insert stems of flowers.

MODIFY BRIDAL COUPLE. Paint dress of bride with thinned pink royal icing. Pipe tiny red dot flowers for bouquet. Brush hair of groom's figure with shaved white chalk to add gray streaks.

Prepare the two-layer tiers

Bake, fill and ice a 15" x 4" and a 12" x 3" hexagon, and an 8" x 3" round tier. For satellite cake, bake, fill and ice 9" x 4" hexagon. Assemble main cake on cake board with pillars and plates. Divide top tier into sixths, using pillars as guide, and mark at base. Transfer pattern for "40" to middle tier. Make your own patterns for scallop design on sides of base and middle tiers.

Decorate the cake

ON SATELLITE CAKE, pull up two tube 504 upright shells at each corner. Complete base border with tube 17 shells. Pipe large ruffly garlands with tube 78. Pipe tube 17 double curved shells for top border, then add two touching curved shells at points of garlands. Attach candy hearts with icing, then border with tube 2 beading.

ON BASE TIER OF MAIN CAKE, pipe a tube 17 bottom shell border. Pull up an upright shell at each corner with tube 504. Following scallop pattern, pipe tube 78 garlands. At top of tier, drop double tube 14 strings, then add a tube 17 top shell border. Edge separator plate with tube 14. Outline "40" with tube 2, then add tube 1 piping gel dots.

ON MIDDLE TIER, pipe a tube 17 base shell border. Following pattern, pipe tube 78 garlands. Do curved shell double top border with tube 17. Edge separator plate with tube 14.

ON TOP TIER, write names with tube 2. Pull up with tube 504 upright shells at marks. Top with tube 16 rosettes and do bottom and top shell borders with same tube.

Complete the picture

Attach candy hearts to tiers with icing. Set bouquet within lower pillars, prepared ornament within upper pillars. On the reception table, attach stairway to link the two cakes and arrange cherub musicians. Set bridge on cake top and pose couple. Add more flowers to trim cake. The main cake will serve 146 guests, cut in wedding cake-sized pieces. Present the satellite cake to the anniversary couple.

Happy first anniversary!

A single tall taper on a luscious chocolate cake brightens the first anniversary celebration. The lacy paper fans make this simple cake very important—and are appropriate for this "paper" anniversary.

DO TRIMS AHEAD. Pipe quick drop flowers in royal icing with tube 30. Add tube 2 centers and dry.

The lacy fans are easy to make. For each fan you will need a 10″ square paper doily. Fold into 1″ pleats, then fold the tightly pleated strip in half to form a half-circle fan.

BAKE AND DECORATE the cake.

Two-layer base tier is a 12″ hexagon, top tier is a single-layer 6″ hexagon. Fill and ice the tiers, then assemble on a cake board 2″ larger all around than the cake.

On base tier, pipe all borders with tube 18 shells. On top tier, pull up two tube 18 upright shells at each corner. Complete borders with tube 16 shells. On center front panel, press a 1″ heart cookie cutter. Print tube 1 message within heart, then border with tube 2 shells. Write couples' names on two adjacent panels with same tube.

COMPLETE THE PICTURE. Tape or

staple ribbon loops on cake board in center of each panel of base tier. Bend the base of a folded fan so fan is about 4″ high, and tape or staple on top of ribbons. Continue until each panel is centered by a fan.

On top tier, insert a taper in center of tier. Bend bases of two folded fans so fans are 3″ high. Attach in front and behind taper with toothpicks, trimming bases as necessary. Now attach clusters of drop flowers at centers of all fans with icing. At serving time, present the top tier to the anniversary couple. Remove fans from base tier and serve cake to 20 party guests.

Gifts of aluminum for the 10th

Who would guess that this imposing centerpiece was easy to decorate? Use your fountain with its filigree frame on top of a simple square cake to give it height and sparkling light. The glittering flowers you can quickly make from aluminum foil—the cherub stands on an aluminum tart pan and even the cake board is covered with foil.

MAKE FLOWERS FIRST. Use an assembly line method for these speedy blooms. Fold a strip of heavy duty foil into quarters (four thicknesses). Press with a cookie cutter to make 2″ circles. Cut the circles out (each will be four thicknesses) and fringe all around

with a scissors. Make stems from florists' wire. Bend a tiny hook in end of each and pull through center of flower. Top with a tube 7 ball of royal icing. Lay flowers on tray to dry as you decorate cake.

BAKE A TWO-LAYER 14″ square cake. Fill and ice, then place on 16″ foil-covered cake board. Edge top and bottom with tube 17 shells. Drop tube 14 strings over base border and top with stars. Pipe tube 14 scallops and stars over top border. Write names on cake side with tube 2. Lightly press an 8″ cake circle in center of cake to imprint. Push in a circle of ten ¼″ dowel rods, then clip off level with top of cake. Set a 10″ cake circle on

top of cake to support fountain.

ADD FINAL TOUCHES. Set fountain on cake circle, then slip Filigree frame over it. Twist stems of flowers through frame. Trace a 1″ heart cutter on stiff paper for two hearts. Cut out, print tube 1 message, edge with beading, then attach to hands of cupid with icing. Use icing to secure cupid to pan.

Insert a flower spike into each corner of cake, midway on side. Arrange clusters of flowers in spikes. Turn on the fountain and wait for applause! Serve your glittering centerpiece to 42 party guests.

For a January anniversary . . . a Carnation cake

If they were married in January, use the fluffy carnation, January's flower, to trim the celebration cake. These large handsome flowers will give importance to any cake—here we've posed them on a three-tier creation that's as beautiful as a wedding cake.

ASSEMBLE YOUR ACCESSORIES
Four 5" Corinthian pillars
Two 10" separator plates
Plastic angel heads
Angelino

Make trims in advance
The oval and heart-shaped plaques that spell out the message are cut from gum paste. Use patterns in the Appendix. Roll out gum paste ⅛" thick and cut ovals, support, and heart using patterns. Dry heart on 16" curved form, other pieces flat. Trim large oval for top ornament with tube 14 shells and number, tube 18 fleur-de-lis. Secure plastic angel heads to plaque with a small piece of gum paste dipped in egg white. Attach triangular support to oval base the same way, and add a 1½" strip of gum paste in front of support. Edge smaller oval with tube 13 curved shells and write names with tube 2. On heart, pipe tube 2 beaded edge and script.

Pipe the flowers
Use royal icing for the carnations. Pipe a tube 12 ball on a number 9 nail. Stiffen icing and pipe tube 104 ruffled petals with a jiggling motion, starting at top center and moving down side of the ball to cover it completely. Pipe a few of the flowers on florists' wire stems. First make a tube 12 calyx, dry and pipe a ball on top of it. Dry again, then pipe petals, holding wire stem as you would a flower nail. Pipe long slender tube 67 leaves on wires.

Prepare the tiers
Bake, fill and ice two-layer tiers— 16", 12" and 8". Make layers for two lower tiers 2" high, for top tier, 1½" high. Assemble with pillars and plates. Divide 8" tier in eighths and mark near base. Connect marks with scallops. Divide 12" tier into twelfths and mark near top edge. Divide 16" tier into twelfths and mark midway on side.

Decorate the cake
ON BOTTOM TIER, secure heart to center front with icing. Pipe and over-pipe scrolls with tube 16 using marks as guides. Do bottom curved shell border with tube 19. Pipe reverse shell top border with tube 17.

ON MIDDLE TIER, pipe scroll and fleur-de-lis design with tube 17. Use tube 19 for base shell border, tube 17 for top border.

ON TOP TIER, pipe base shell border with tube 16. Use the same tube for the side trim. Pipe zigzag scallops with a scroll below each. Add fleurs-de-lis, then over-pipe the scallops with a tube 13 line. Add a tube 16 top shell border.

Complete the picture
Secure large oval to support with small balls of gum paste dipped in egg white. Attach smaller oval to pillar the same way and add a plastic Angelino at base. Arrange flowers, securing with icing, and trim with leaves. Serve wedding cake-sized pieces of two lower tiers to 186. Present the top tier to the anniversary couple.

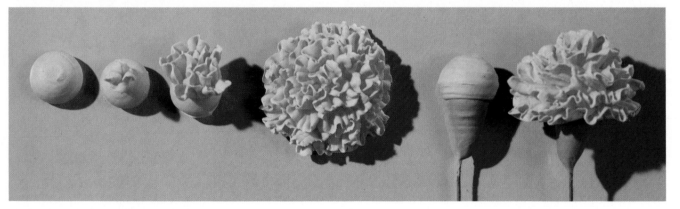

Is theirs a July anniversary?
Grace the cake with water lilies

July's flower, newly formed in gum paste, trims this delicate cake of unusual construction.

MAKE THE FLOWERS. Read the booklet that comes with the Flower garden set for basic instructions. For large lily, clip the legs off the bowl of the Angel fountain and cover inside of bowl with gum paste. Dry. Cut petals with daffodil cutter, separate into three, roll to curl and secure around outside of bowl. Cut ten leaves with the large violet cutter, roll to elongate, and attach for second row of petals. For third row of petals, cut eight leaves with the lily leaf cutter. Roll to enlarge, curl on a soft sponge, then cut a ½" slit at base of leaf. Cross these two points to cup petal and secure to base of flower.

For small lilies, cut three shapes with the small daisy cutter. Roll each to enlarge, curl on a soft sponge, then assemble as shown on page 18 of booklet. Pipe tube 1 royal icing stamens. Cut plaque, using pattern, and dry on a 10" curved form. Pipe names and beading with tube 1.

Cut a 7" circle from corrugated cardboard and cover with foil for plate for upper tier. Cover a 4½" circle with foil for base. Glue four 5" Corinthian pillars, set close together, on base and plate.

BAKE A 10½" RING CAKE and a single-layer 6" cake and cover with poured fondant. Assemble tiers on serving tray, using prepared pillars. Divide top tier into sixths, mark about ½" down from top. Divide lower tier into tenths, mark 1" up from base.

DECORATE THE CAKE. Pipe tube 16 base shell borders on both tiers. On base tier, pipe tube 103 curved ruffles below marks, then tube 16 garlands and fleurs-de-lis and tube 3 strings and hearts. Use same tubes for border on upper tier. Attach lilies and plaque with royal icing and serve to 18 admiring party guests.

Lacy and lovely for the 13th

Pretty as a wedding cake, and lavished with lace, the traditional gift for the 13th anniversary.

MAKE TRIMS AHEAD. Pipe royal icing drop flowers with tubes 224, 225 and 131. Mount some on wire stems to form a bouquet. Cut two paper hearts, using cookie cutter as pattern. Pipe names with tube 1 and glue hearts to hands of cherub figure. Trim with flowers and beading. Prepare a cake board for upper tier by tracing a 9" hexagon pan on strong cardboard. Cover with foil and glue on six stud plates. Using patterns, pipe about 100 lace pieces with tube 1s. Pipe wings with tube 1. When dry, turn over and over-pipe main lines.

BAKE, FILL AND ICE the two-layer tiers—a 12" round and a 9" hexagon. Place 12" tier on serving tray and lightly mark position of twist legs by pressing with prepared hexagon board. Transfer scalloped pattern to cake top. Assemble tiers with six twist legs from Crystal clear set. Divide side of lower tier into twelfths and mark 1" down from top edge. Make a second series of marks for garlands about 1½" up from base. Drop string guidelines. On upper tier mark "13" pattern.

ON BASE TIER, pipe a tube 16 bottom shell border, then zigzag garlands. Trim with double tube 2 string and tube 13 rosettes. Pipe tube 1 cornelli lace, tube 2 beading.

ON TOP TIER, outline "13" with tube 2 and dot with tube 1s. Pipe a tube 13 bottom shell border, tube 4 bulb borders at corners and top edge. Drop string guidelines for zigzag garlands. Pipe with tube 16 and add double tube 2 string, tube 13 rosettes. Glue Winged angels to pillars and place bouquet. Set cherub on top and trim cake with flowers. Add tube 65 leaves. Attach lace last with dots of icing. Serve this exquisite cake to 34 party guests.

145

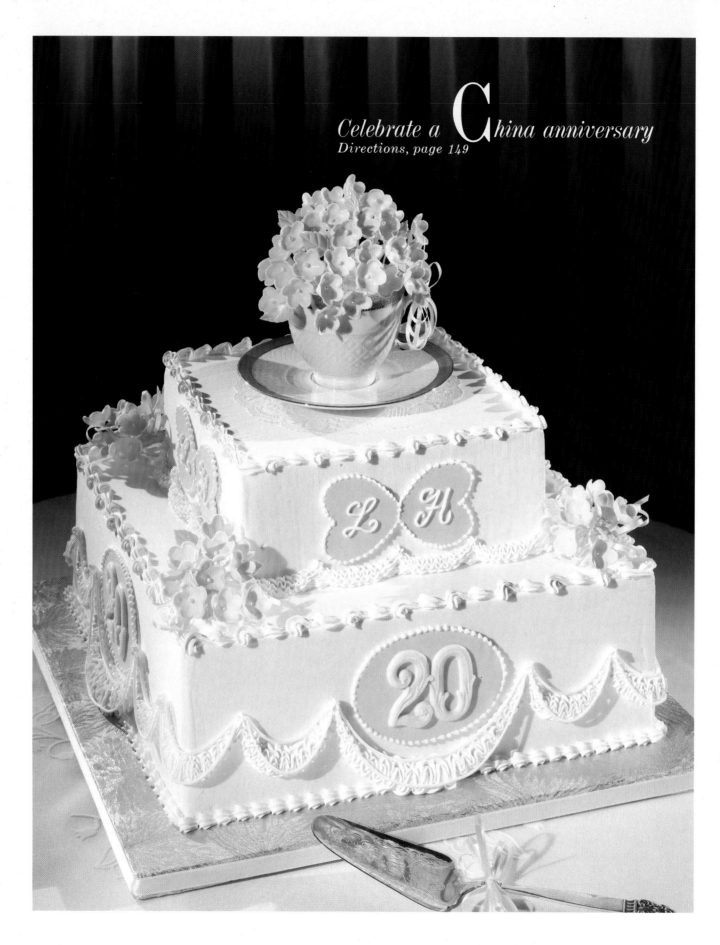

Celebrate a **C***hina anniversary*
Directions, page 149

A golden cake for the **50**th
Directions, page 149

Surprise them with a "jade" cake on their 35th anniversary

The 35th is the anniversary when guests present gifts of jade, so this lovely cake is adorned with icing facsimiles of that stone.

DO HEART AND OVAL JADE stones in Color Flow. Outline with tube 2, flow in thinned icing, dry and edge with tube 1. Do oval plaque for top of tier by outlining with tube 5 and flowing in with a thicker icing, the consistency of honey, for a rounded look. Dry thoroughly. Edge small oval and heart shapes with tube 2 beading.

Bake a 12″ x 4″ two-layer round tier and a 7″ x 9″ oval single-layer tier. Fill the 12″ tier, ice both tiers and assemble. Divide side of lower tier into sixths. Transfer patterns to both tiers.

On 12″ tier, pipe bottom border with tube 18. Just below each marked side design pipe three radiating shells and a star, then complete shell border. Pipe a tube 18 reverse shell border on top. Pipe side designs, using tube 18 for center part, tube 16 for outer scrolls.

Pipe frame on oval tier. Secure oval plaque in center, then pipe radiating tube 16 lines around it. Border plaque with tube 16 shells. Pipe outer scrolls with tube 13. Do fancy numbers with tube 1. Pipe tube 16 top and bottom shell borders, then pipe side designs with same tube. Attach jade stones with

dots of icing. This stunning cake serves party-size pieces to 28 guests.

Here is a list of anniversary gifts that will suggest cake trims:

1st—paper	14th—ivory
2nd—cotton	15th—crystal
3rd—leather	20th—china
4th—fruit, flowers	25th—silver
5th—wood	30th—pearl
6th—iron	35th—jade
7th—copper	40th—ruby
8th—bronze	45th—sapphire
9th—pottery	50th—gold
10th—aluminum	55th—emerald
11th—steel	60th—diamond
12th—silk	75th—diamond

A golden cake for the 50th
shown on page 147

An impressive cake for an important occasion. Heaped with autumn-toned mums, this golden cake is surprisingly easy to decorate. The flowers are piped in a quick, easy method.

MAKE SHAGGY MUMS in royal icing on wax paper. You'll need about 65. Pipe a tube 199 mound. Holding tube 233 straight up, pipe hairlike petals on top of mound. Circle with more petals, holding tube at 45° angle. Finish with a final row of petals near base of mound, holding tube almost parallel to paper. Dry.

BAKE TWO-LAYER TIERS—14" x 4" square, 10" x 4" round and 6" x 3" round. Fill and ice with buttercream. Assemble with 5" Grecian pillars and 8" separator plates. Place 10" round tier slightly to rear of base tier. Divide each side of base tier into fourths and mark at top edge. Mark corresponding scallops on tier top with a cookie cutter. Divide middle tier into 16ths, top tier into 12ths and mark at top edge.

ON BASE TIER, pipe a tube 32 bottom star border. Fill in marked scallops with tube 3 lattice and edge with tube 3. Drop tube 3 guidelines from these scallops on tier sides and cover with tube 5 garlands. Edge top of tier with tube 22 stars.

ON MIDDLE TIER, pipe tube 17 stars at base. Drop two rows of tube 3 string from top edge and do shell border at top with tube 17. Edge separator plate with tube 3 zigzag.

ON 6" TIER, pipe base border with tube 17 stars. Drop guidelines from top edge and cover with tube 3 garland. Trim with tube 3 string. Edge top with tube 17 stars.

Pipe a mound of icing within pillars, set on mums, then drape graceful "lei" of flowers on two lower tiers, attaching each with dots of icing. Set ornament on cake top and circle with mums. Add more flowers to top tier. Set anniversary couple on base tier. Two lower tiers serve 146 wedding cake-sized pieces.

Celebrate a china anniversary
shown on page 146

Make this exquisite cake for their 20th anniversary, when the guests present gifts of china to the honored couple. Porcelain-like gum paste flowers are arranged on the tiers and fill a china cup and saucer that's a gift, too. Even the plaques on the tier sides have a china-smooth finish.

MAKE FLOWERS FIRST. This can be done weeks ahead of decorating day. Tint gum paste in dainty pastels. Roll out a small portion to 1/16" thickness and use the violet cutter (from the Flower garden set) to cut several blossoms. Work with one flower at a time, keeping others covered under a glass bowl to prevent drying out. Place the flower on a piece of foam toweling. Cup each petal by pressing from the tip to the center with the rounded end of a stick. Make a tiny hole in the center of the flower. Pull the stem of an artificial stamen through the hole. Wind stamen stem around a length of fine florists' wire, then wrap completed stem with floral tape. Stick in styrofoam to dry.

To make leaves, roll out gum paste to 1/16" thickness. Cut leaves with the small violet cutter, then press into a leaf mold to vein. Lay leaf upside down, dip the end of a length of fine florists' wire in egg white and gently press to leaf. Pinch the bottom of the leaf around the wire and furl the leaf with your fingers. Lay on cornstarch-dusted surface to dry.

WEDGE A PIECE OF STYROFOAM into a china cup. Stick stems of flowers into styrofoam to arrange a bouquet. Make four more little bouquets by twisting stems together. Tie with ribbon bows.

TO MAKE PLAQUES, roll out tinted gum paste to ⅛" thickness and cut out, using patterns in the appendix. Cut out "20" from untinted gum paste. When dry, write couples' initials on heart plaque with royal icing. Attach "20" to oval with icing and add decorative curves with tube 2.

BAKE AND DECORATE the cake. Bake two-layer square tiers—12" x 4" and 8" x 3". Fill, ice and assemble on foil-covered cake board. Divide each side of 8" tier into fourths and mark 1" up from base. On base tier, make marks midway on side, 1" in from each corner. Make a second series of marks 2" away from first.

Pipe a tube 16 shell border at base of both tiers. On base tier, drop guidelines, then pipe zigzag garlands with tube 16. Trim with double tube 2 strings. Add a reverse shell top border.

On top tier, pipe tube 15 garlands from mark to mark and top with stars. Pipe a tube 15 reverse shell top border. Secure plaques to tier sides with mounds of royal icing. Edge with tube 2 beading.

Lay a doily on cake top and set cup and saucer in position. Push four Flower spikes into corners of base tier. Place small bouquets in them. Your pretty cake is finished! Serve to 48 party guests.

A centerpiece for a Golden anniversary

This is the cake to make for a grand celebration of 50 years of married love. It's ablaze with 50 candles, brightened by 50 roses and altogether spectacular. This design could be adapted for a magnificent wedding cake, too.

ASSEMBLE YOUR ACCESSORIES
Five anniversary emblems
Five 7½" Corinthian pillars, sprayed gold
Two 14" separator plates (from Crystal clear set)
Five stud plates
Cake board, 22" round of plywood or masonite
50 candles
50 Push-in candle holders
Gold artificial leaves

Do trims ahead of time

MAKE THE FLOWERS in advance—then trimming the cake with simple but lavish looking borders will go quickly. Make 50 two-tone jubilee roses with tube 126 as described on page 84. Also make many smaller jubilee roses, sweet peas and rosebuds with tube 104. Dry, then mount three large roses on wire stems. Pipe royal icing spikes on the backs of the rest and on most of the smaller roses.

SPRAY PILLARS GOLD and dry. Glue five stud plates to the flat sides of each of two 14" separator plates from Crystal Clear Cake Divider set. Dry, then paint with thinned royal icing to match icing on cake and dry again.

Prepare the tiers

Bake round tiers—18" x 6" is three layers high. 14" x 4", 10" x 4" and 6" x 3" tiers are two layers high. Fill, ice and assemble on foil-covered board. Insert ½" dowel rods in the two lower tiers for support and ¼" dowels in the 10" tier, all clipped off level with tier tops. (See page 166.)

Divide base tier into fifths, using pillars as guide. Transfer scallop pattern at each division. Divide 14" tier into fifteenths and mark 1" up from base. Divide 10" tier in tenths and mark midway on side. Divide top tier into fifths and mark near top edge.

Decorate the cake

ON BASE TIER, pipe a tube 17 base shell border on 18" tier. Pipe zigzag garlands on marked patterns with tube 15. Pipe a pair of tube 18 zigzag garlands topped with a fleur-de-lis at base of cake between the scallop patterns. Add tube 20 reverse shell top border and tube 17 reverse shells around separator plate.

On 14" TIER pipe tube 16 base shell border. Pipe tube 17 zigzag garlands from mark to mark. Top every third intersection with a tube 18 fleur-de-lis. Add a tube 19 reverse shell top border.

ON 10" TIER, pipe tube 18 base shell border, tube 18 reverse shell top border. Pipe a tube 18 fleur-de-lis at every other mark.

ON TOP TIER, pipe tube 17 borders—shells at base, reverse shells at top.

Attach the flowers to the tiers as pictured with royal icing. Secure a mound of smaller roses, rosebuds and sweet peas to the separator plate, then attach the emblems between the pillars with royal icing. Trim with small roses, rosebuds and sweet peas. Trim all the flowers with gold artificial leaves. Insert candle holders in the sides of the tiers and trim with tube 15 rosettes. Use 20 holders in 18" tier, 15 in 14" tier, ten in 10" tier and five in 6" tier for a total of fifty. Set in candles. The three lower tiers serve wedding-size servings to 288 guests.

CHAPTER EIGHT

Cakes for the Groom... Cakes for Showers

These are the cakes that add so much to the joyful parties that precede the wedding—and to the wedding itself.

SHOWER CAKES are fun to decorate! You can give a hint of the wedding cake-to-come by using the same flowers and type of trim. Or use the favorite colors of the bride-to-be. Bells, bows, hearts and dainty lace are favorite themes—and, of course, parasols to represent the shower of gifts.

GROOM'S CAKES are traditionally cut in wedding cake-sized pieces and daintily boxed. Single girls place them under their pillows to dream on—perhaps to catch a glimpse of a future mate! Or they are presented as souvenirs of the wedding celebration. A groom's cake provides a handsome addition to a sweet table, too. It is usually a rich pound cake or fruit cake iced in chocolate, the better to contrast with the snowy whiteness of the bride's cake.

Chocolate hexagon

Covered with glossy fondant, trimmed with marzipan and a stand-up ornament, this is a delicious show-piece.

PIPE ORNAMENT PIECES on wax paper, using pattern, tube 13 and royal icing. When dry, turn over and pipe again. Construct ornament by attaching pieces with dots of royal icing.

ROLL OUT MARZIPAN and cut 18 small 1″ hearts with a cutter. Use a 2″ cutter to cut 18 circles. Trim off a fourth of the circles, then cut out hearts with a 1″ cutter. Cut a 4½″ circle for top of cake.

BAKE AND FILL a two-layer 12″ hexagon cake. Ice with buttercream, then cover with chocolate poured fondant. Set on cake board. Press circle trims around base of cake. Place circle on top and arrange small hearts around it. Add ornament and cut into 50 servings.

Chocolate Rose

A spray of chocolate roses surrrounds a marzipan plaque. Pipe the roses and buds with tube 104 and chocolate buttercream, then refrigerate until ready to use. Everyone loves chocolate roses!

ROLL OUT MARZIPAN about ⅛″ thick and cut the oval plaque, using pattern in the Appendix.

BAKE AND FILL a 9″ x 13″ two-layer cake. Ice top smoothly and sides thickly with buttercream. Place on cake board, then make a wavy design on sides with a decorating comb. Pipe bottom border with tube 17 rosettes, top border with tube 14 shells. Secure plaque on cake top and edge with tube 14 shells. Pipe names with tube 2. Arrange the roses on mounds of icing, then pipe tube 7 stems with tube 1 thorns. Add tube 67 leaves. Cut into 54 servings.

Golden silk flowers . . .
top an impressive two-tier cake for
the groom. Bake and fill the
two-layer tiers—a 12″ x 4″ round
and a 9″ x 3″ hexagon. Ice with
mocha buttercream and assemble.
Decorating is quickly done with
chocolate buttercream—a nice
contrast in flavors.

ON BASE TIER, divide in twelfths and
mark near bottom. Pull up a tube
19 column at each division.
Complete base border with tube 22
shells. Frame with tube 13 zigzags.
Drop tube 14 strings to connect
columns, then add tube 19
fleurs-de-lis and tube 13 stars. Do
top shell border with tube 17.

ON TOP TIER, pull up tube 19
columns at each corner. Add
fleurs-de-lis with same tube.
Complete bottom border with tube
22 shells. Frame with tube 14
zigzags and scallops. Do top border
with tube 14. We arranged the
flowers in a little brass cricket box
to top the cake. Cut into 90 slices.

A latticed groom's cake

It's easy to decorate this imposing cake—use a pattern press to define the lattice trim.

BAKE A TWO-LAYER 12″ hexagon cake. Fill and ice with buttercream. Place on serving plate. Mark designs on top and sides with a pattern press. Pipe tube 3 lattice to fill designs and frame with tube 14 scrolls. Pipe a triple row of tube 14 shells at base of cake, a double row of shells with same tube at top and side edges. Serves fifty, cut in wedding cake-sized pieces.

A tassel-tied shower cake

This summery cake was planned to harmonize with the wedding cake on page 79, but it will make a pretty centerpiece for any shower.

MAKE SIX-PIECE lattice fence. Cover pattern with wax paper and pipe with tube 2 and royal icing. Overpipe edges for strength. Set aside to dry. Make daisies with tubes 103 and 104 with tube 3 centers. Dry on curved surface. Mount about six daisies on wire stems.

BAKE, FILL AND ICE two-layer round tiers, 12″ and 6″. Assemble on serving tray.

Divide 6″ tier into sixths and mark midway on side. Pipe tube 14 shell border at base, tube 16 shells at top. Pipe a tube 16 garland from mark to mark and center two tube 16 upright shells between each. Drop double tube 2 strings. Top each upright shell with a star piped with tube 16.

Divide 12″ tier into sixths and mark near top edge. Trace oval pattern on side of cake and outline with tube 2 beading. Pipe tube 2 lettering within oval at front of cake. Pipe tube 20 shell border at base, tube 18 shells at top. Pipe a short and a longer tube 16 rope on sides from marks. At ends of rope, pipe tube 2 tassels, overpiping for full effect. Attach daisies with icing and trim with tube 65 leaves.

Attach plastic birds in center of top tier with icing. Plant wired daisies around them. Pipe a line of icing on bottom and one side of two sections of lattice fence. Set sections in position on cake top. Continue with other four sections. Where sections join, pipe tube 3 beading to reinforce. Serve to 28.

154

Bachelor button groom's cake

Set off the deep hues of the flowers with a white cake top, then frame the handsome picture in rich chocolate.

PIPE FLOWERS IN ADVANCE in royal icing. Use a number 2 nail to define size of the flower. Pipe a tube 8 ball in center of nail. With deep-colored icing, pull out a cluster of tube 13 petals in center of ball, holding tube straight up. Change to tube 15 and lighter icing. Circle the first group of petals, then add more rows of petals, slanting tube outward as you approach edge of nail. Dry.

BAKE AND FILL a two-layer 9″ oval cake. Ice top in white buttercream, side chocolate. In centers of long sides of cake, pipe tube 18 fleurs-de-lis. Use the same tube to edge base of cake with stars. At narrow ends of cake, pipe graduated curved shells. Do top border with deeply curved tube 17 shells. Pipe a cluster of tube 4 stems on cake top. Spatula-stripe a cone fitted with tube 65 with deep green icing and fill with paler green. Pull out long slender tube 65 leaves. Arrange the flowers on mounds of icing. Cut into 24 pieces.

An embroidered shower cake

Dainty gum paste blossoms in palest blue trim this cake for the bride-to-be.

MAKE FLOWERS. Use the violet cutter from the Flower garden cutter set and directions on age 97. Mount the flowers on wire stems, twist into a little bouquet and tie with satin ribbon.

BAKE A TWO-LAYER, 8″ round cake. Fill and ice with buttercream, then cover with poured fondant. Mark a 4″ circle in center of cake. Edge with tube 2 beading. From circle outward, cover entire surface with tube ls freehand embroidery. Finish with a tube 7 bulb border. Set bouquet on cake top and serve to ten shower guests.

Bells and parasols . . .

trim the pretty shower cake (at left) delicately piped in pink.

PIPE TINY APPLE BLOSSOMS in royal icing with tube 101s. When dry, use the flowers to trim the petite bell ornament and small plastic parasols. Attach with icing.

BAKE, FILL AND ICE a 10″ two-layer cake. Make scallop pattern for cake top by folding an 8″ circle of parchment paper into sixteenths. Cut curve on outer edge, then transfer to cake.

PIPE BASE BORDER with tube 10 balls. Pipe contrasting trim with tube 5. On top of cake, outline scallops with tube 2 beading. Drop triple tube 1 strings from top edge. Pipe a tube 4 top ball border, add contrasting trim with same tube. Set ornament on cake and push in handles of parasols. Serve this dainty treat to 14 party guests.

A sweetheart shower cake

(Above) Two little doves hold a garland of blossoms on top of this love-shaped cake.

PIPE FLOWERS in royal icing. Use tube 102 for apple blossoms and rosebuds, tube 101s for tiny apple blossoms.

BAKE, FILL AND ICE a two-layer 9″ heart cake. Divide each side in eighths and mark near base. From each mark, pull up a tube 199 upright shell to form columns. Frame bases with tube 20 and "e" motion. Connect tops of columns with tube 2 dropped guidelines, then pipe "e" motion garlands with tube 14. Pipe corresponding scallops on cake top with the same tube.

Pipe a thick curve of icing on cake top to define flower garland. At ends, pipe tube 2 stems. Press in flowers, then add tube 65 leaves. Attach doves at ends of garland and pipe tube 1 ribbons from their beaks.

Finish cake with shell-motion hearts. Use tube 9 for hearts at base, tube 7 for top. Serve to twelve shower guests.

A violet nosegay

Simple and sweet and simply beautiful for a springtime shower!

DO TRIMS IN ADVANCE. Pipe violets in royal icing with tube 59° on a number 7 nail. With light pressure, move tube out and back from center of nail to make a ½" petal. Pipe two more petals the same way, then two shorter ¼" petals. Pipe two stamens in center with tube 1. When dry, mount on wire stems.

Pipe tube 70 leaves on wire. To form nosegay, twist stems of flowers together, then add a frame of leaves. Wrap stems with floral tape and tie with a blue satin ribbon.

Pipe lace pieces, using pattern, royal icing and tube 1.

BAKE AND FILL a two-layer 8" round cake. Ice with buttercream, then cover with rolled fondant. For handkerchief effect, cut a 7⅛"

square of wax paper. Center on cake top and trace with a toothpick.

Pipe tube 1 cornelli lace from base of cake to edge of handkerchief. Pipe a tube 7 bottom ball border. Edge handkerchief with tube 1 beading. Attach lace pieces by piping a tiny line at outer edge of beading then setting lace piece in position. Set nosegay on cake and serve to ten shower guests.

Flowering lattice hearts

Frilly, feminine, trimmed with roses! This shower confection is easy to serve, too.

PIPE FLOWERS IN ADVANCE in royal icing. For top of cake, pipe tube 102 rosebuds and roses. When dry, mount on wire stems. Pipe tube 67 leaves on wire. Make two little clusters of rosebuds and leaves for hearts. Twist stems together and wrap with floral tape. Make a larger cluster of roses and leaves. For bottom border, pipe tiny roses with tube 101s.

MAKE LATTICE HEARTS, using heart minicake pan as mold. Tape pattern for center openings on pan, then grease pan with solid white vegetable shortening. Pipe lattice in royal icing with tube 2, stopping ½" above base of pan. Use tube 14 to pipe a shell border around base of hearts and curved scrolls around opening. When dry, place pan in warm oven a few minutes, then carefully push off hearts.

BAKE, FILL AND ICE a two-layer 9" x 13" cake. Starting 1" in from corners, divide long sides of cake into fifths and mark ½" below top edge. Starting 1" in from corners, divide short sides into thirds and mark ½" below top edge. Repeat markings on top of cake, 1" in from edge.

Pipe tube 21 garlands around base of cake and frame with tube 14 zigzags. Following marks, pipe tube 16 scallops on side and top. Over-pipe with an "e" motion. Fill in area between scallops with tube 2 dots. Place a tiny rose between each base garland and trim with tube 65 leaves. Position lattice hearts on cake top, then push in rosebud and rose clusters. Serve this pretty showpiece to 24 shower guests.

A shower of violets

The prettiest, wittiest cake ever decorated for a spring-time shower! Pastel parasols perch on a cake trimmed with violets. Pipe the violets and make the gum paste parasols in advance—then the cake is very quickly decorated.

MOLD PARASOLS. Roll out gum paste and tint. Use plastic ball molds to mold the parasols. Mold three parasols over 4½" molds, one full and one half-parasol over 3" molds.

Cut parasols, using patterns, and smooth over molds. Make a tiny hole in center of each for handle. Cut 6" long handles from stiff florists' wire and paint with thinned royal icing to match gum paste. Insert handles into dried parasols, securing with royal icing. Trim with ribbon bows.

PIPE VIOLETS with tubes 101 and 1 in royal icing. When dry, mount most flowers on wire stems. Pipe tube 65 leaves on wire stems.

BAKE, FILL AND ICE a 9" x 13" two-layer sheet cake. Pipe shell borders at base and top with tube 17. Insert handles of three umbrellas on top of cake, sprinkle violets beneath them and attach wired violets with dots of icing. Set smaller whole and half-parasols on side of cake, securing with icing. Trim with violets. Cluster violets on sides of cake, adding tube 65 leaves. Serve to 24 party guests.

Zinnias light up a shower

Brilliant bouquet zinnias follow curves of this petal-shaped cake to make an elegant centerpiece for the shower party.

PIPE THE ZINNIAS. These showy flowers are a full 2½" across! Use boiled or royal icing and a number 8 flower nail. Line the nail with foil and lightly grease the foil. Cover entire top surface with icing, then pipe a tube 10 ball in center.

Starting at outer edge, circle the nail with tube 101s petals. Continue, lifting the tube as you near center. Change to tube 349 for the last two circles of petals. Pipe a cluster of tube 1 stamens in center. Lift foil off nail to dry.

BAKE AND FILL a two-layer 12" petal cake. Ice smoothly in buttercream and set on serving tray. Lightly press a 6" round pan in center of cake top to define pattern.

DECORATE CAKE. Pipe a tube 16 stem in center of each curve on side of cake. Pipe a tube 16 bottom shell border, then pipe deeply curved tube 21 shells. Outline curves on top edge with tube 18 swirls and pipe a rosette in center. Using marked circle as guide, pipe tube 16 swirls. Attach flowers on mounds of icing, then pipe tube 68 leaves. Cut each curve of the cake into three pieces to serve 24.

CHAPTER NINE

All you need to know

to create a Wonderful Wedding Cake

ARE YOU A NOVICE decorator about to decorate your very first wedding cake? Take courage! Study this chapter and you'll learn just how to bake and ice the tiers, the all-important assembly, and the correct ways to carry your creation to the reception site, then cut and serve it. Expert ways of working with piped flowers are clearly described. It even shows you how to put together exciting stairway cakes. Just use basic decorating techniques and you'll be assured of success.

FOR EXPERIENCED DECORATORS, this chapter provides a valuable refresher course. Don't miss the tips shared by our staff of professional decorators. They'll save you time and effort—and help you make your bridal cakes more beautiful.

Tested icing recipes

Here are all the recipes you need to decorate the cakes in this book. All have been tested and retested. For most of the cakes, we recommend covering the cake with buttercream. This is a rich, well-liked icing that goes on smoothly. For borders and other trim, boiled icing is excellent. It pipes clear well-defined shapes, flows easily from the tube and has a nice glossy finish. By using boiled icing, you avoid the too-rich effect that would result from using buttercream for heavy borders.

PLEASE NOTE: When making *boiled* or *royal icings*, make sure that no grease gets into the icing. Even a speck of grease will break these icings down. Do not use plastic utensils. It is very difficult to keep plastic grease-free.

FOR MOST FLOWERS, stiffen the icing by stirring in additional confectioners' sugar.

TO PIPE LEAVES AND STRING, thin the icing by adding one teaspoon of white corn syrup to each cup of icing. Try practicing a few strings and leaves—if necessary, add more corn syrup. Piping gel may be substituted for corn syrup.

TO TINT pastel shades, add a few drops of liquid food color. For deep colors, apply paste color with a toothpick, very sparingly. Remember, the color of tinted buttercream will deepen in a few hours.

Wilton snow-white buttercream

This is a pure white, versatile and delicious icing. We recommend it for covering the cake, piping borders and for cake-top flowers. Tints to clear pretty colors.

   ⅔ cup water
   4 tablespoons meringue powder
   1¼ cups solid white shortening, room temperature
   11½ cups confectioners' sugar, sifted
   ¾ teaspoon salt
   ¼ teaspoon butter flavoring
   ½ teaspoon almond flavoring
   ½ teaspoon clear vanilla flavoring

Combine water and meringue powder and whip at high speeds until peaks form. Add four cups sugar, one cup at a time, beating after each addition at low speed. Alternately add shortening and remainder of sugar. Add salt and flavorings and beat at low speed until smooth. May be stored, well covered, in refrigerator for several weeks, then brought to room temperature and rebeaten. Yield: 8 cups. Recipe may be cut in half or doubled.

FOR CHOCOLATE BUTTERCREAM, add 8 tablespoons of cocoa and 2 tablespoons of water to one-half of the recipe above. Add these ingredients before beating in sugar.

FOR MOCHA BUTTERCREAM, dissolve 6½ tablespoons instant coffee in 4 tablespoons of hot water. Cool, then add to one-half of recipe above before beating in sugar. For more attractive color, tint with 5 drops of red liquid food color.

Wilton chocolate buttercream

A delicious, light chocolate-colored icing, ideal for icing the cake and piping borders. To pipe flowers mix 1 cup of confectioners' sugar with 1 cup of the finished icing. For a darker flower, add 3 tablespoons of cocoa and ⅔ cup of confectioners' sugar to one cup of icing.

   ⅓ cup butter
   ⅓ cup solid white shortening
   ½ cup cocoa
   ½ cup milk
   1 pound confectioners' sugar, sifted
   5 tablespoons cool milk or cream
   1 teaspoon vanilla
   ⅛ teaspoon salt

Cream butter and shortening. Mix cocoa and ½ cup milk and add to creamed mixture. Beat in sugar, one cup at a time, blending well after each addition and scraping sides and bottom of bowl frequently. Add cool milk, vanilla and salt and beat at high speed until light and fluffy. Keep icing covered with a lid or damp cloth and store in refrigerator. Bring to room temperature and rebeat to original consistency.
Yield: 3⅔ cups.

Wilton boiled icing—meringue

Excellent and easy to use for borders. You may use it to pipe roses and sweet peas, but flowers are more fragile than those piped of royal icing. Not suitable for covering the cake. Keep utensils grease free!

Mixture One:

2 cups granulated sugar
½ cup warm water
¼ teaspoon cream of tartar

Mixture Two:

½ cup warm water
4 tablespoons meringue powder
3½ cups sifted confectioners' sugar

Combine ingredients in Mixture One in a 1½-quart heavy saucepan. Place over high heat and stir until all sugar crystals are dissolved. After this, do not stir. Insert candy thermometer and wash down sides of pan with a pastry brush dipped in hot water. At 240°F, remove from heat.

Meanwhile, prepare Mixture Two. Whip meringue powder and water about seven minutes or until fluffy. Add confectioners' sugar and whip at low speed about three minutes. Slowly pour hot syrup (Mixture One) into batch and whip at high speed until light and very fluffy. Use immediately or refrigerate in a tightly closed container for weeks. Bring to room temperature and rebeat to use again. Yield: 6 cups.

Wilton boiled icing—egg white

This marshmallow flavored icing is fine for covering the cake. Do not use for borders or flowers. Any trace of grease will break it down.

2 cups granulated sugar
½ cup water
¼ teaspoon cream of tartar
4 egg whites, room temperature
1½ cups confectioners' sugar, sifted

Combine granulated sugar, water and cream of tartar in a 1½ quart heavy saucepan. Place over high heat and stir until all sugar crystals are dissolved. Wash down sides of pan with a pastry brush dipped in hot water. After this, do not stir. At 240°F, remove from heat.

Meanwhile, whip egg whites 7 minutes at high speed. Add boiled sugar mixture slowly, beat 3 minutes at high speed. Turn to

second speed, gradually add confectioners' sugar, beat 7 minutes more at high speed. Rebeating will not restore texture. Yield: 3½ cups.

Wilton royal icing—meringue

Perfect for piping all flowers. After drying, they may be mounted on wire stems, or spikes may be piped on backs to secure to cake sides. Excellent for lace, free-standing lattice and fine string work. Do not use for covering the cake.

3 level tablespoons meringue powder
3½ ounces warm water
1 pound confectioners' sugar, sifted
½ teaspoon cream of tartar

Combine ingredients, mixing slowly, then beat at high speed for 7 to 10 minutes. Keep covered with a damp cloth, icing dries quickly. Store, tightly covered, in refrigerator for weeks. Bring to room temperature and rebeat to use again. Yield: 3½ cups.

Wilton royal icing—egg white

This is an even stronger icing than the one above, and may be used for the same purposes. Use at once, for rebeating will not restore texture. Dries too hard for covering the cake. Keep grease-free!

3 egg whites, room temperature
1 pound confectioners' sugar, sifted
½ teaspoon cream of tartar

Combine ingredients, beat at high speed 7 to 10 minutes. Dries quickly—keep covered with a damp cloth while using. Rebeating will not restore texture. Yield: 3 cups.

Wilton quick poured fondant

For a shiny, grease-free surface that sets off delicate trim.

6 cups confectioners' sugar, sifted
4 ounces water
2 tablespoons white corn syrup
1 teaspoon almond flavoring

Combine water and corn syrup. Add to sugar in a saucepan and stir over low heat until well-mixed and heated to 92°F, thin enough to be poured, but thick enough so it won't run off the cake. Add flavor and color, if desired.

To COVER CAKE, ice smoothly with buttercream and let icing crust. Place cake on cooling rack with a

cookie sheet beneath it. Pour fondant over iced cake, flowing from center and moving out in a circular motion. Touch up sides with a spatula. Excess fondant can be stored, tightly covered, in refrigerator for weeks. Reheat to use again. Yield: 4 cups, enough to cover a 10″ round cake. Recipe may be doubled or tripled.

CHOCOLATE POURED FONDANT. Follow recipe of Quick Poured Fondant, but increase amount of water by 1 ounce. After fondant is heated, stir in 3 ounces of melted, unsweetened chocolate, then add flavoring.

Wilton rolled fondant

Give yourself a little time to practice and you'll find you can cover a cake with rolled fondant in just a few minutes. It gives a beautiful satin-smooth finish with softly rounded edges. *Use only a firm pound cake or fruit cake* for this covering.

½ ounce gelatin
¼ cup water
2 pounds confectioners' sugar, sifted three times
2 tablespoons solid white shortening
½ cup glucose
¾ ounce glycerine
2 or 3 drops clear flavoring
liquid food color, as desired

Heat gelatin and water in a small pan until just dissolved. Put sifted sugar in a large bowl and make a depression in the center. Add shortening, glucose and glycerine to the dissolved gelatin and heat until shortening is just melted. Mix well. Pour mixture into depression in sugar and mix with your hands to a dough-like consistency.

Transfer to a smooth surface sprayed with nonstick pan release and lightly dusted with cornstarch. Knead until smooth and pliable. Add flavoring and color while kneading. If too soft, knead in a little sifted confectioners' sugar. If too stiff, add boiling water, a drop at a time.

Use immediately or store in an airtight container at room temperature for up to a week. If storing longer, refrigerate and bring to room temperature before kneading and rolling out. Will cover a 14″ round or 12″ square cake. Recipe may be doubled.

Wilton gum paste

Baroque trims, flowers that look like fresh-cut blooms and lifelike little figures are all achievable with this pliable substance.

1 heaping tablespoon glucose

3 tablespoons warm water

1 tablespoon Gum-tex™ or tragacanth gum

1 pound sifted confectioners' sugar (or more)

Heat glucose and water till just warm. Mix Gum-tex with 1 cup of the sugar and add to glucose mixture. Mix well. Gradually knead in enough sugar until you have used about ¾ pound.

Gum paste handles best when aged, so store in a plastic bag at least overnight, then break off a piece and work in more sugar until pliable but not sticky. Always keep well-covered.

TO STORE for a length of time, place gun paste in a plastic bag and then in a covered container to prevent drying. It will keep several months.

TO TINT, add color directly to the gum paste by applying a small amount of paste food color with a toothpick. Knead to spread tint evenly throughout.

TO ROLL OUT GUM PASTE, dust your work surface well with cornstarch. Work a small piece of gum paste and roll it out with a small rolling pin, also dusted with cornstarch.

TO MOLD GUM PASTE, follow the directions that come with the molds.

Wilton hard candy

In about ten minutes you'll turn out perfect jewel-like little shapes.

1 cup granulated cane sugar

⅓ cup hot water

⅓ cup light corn syrup

½ teaspoon liquid food color

½ teaspoon oil-based flavoring

Brush hard candy molds with vegetable oil and lay on cookie sheet.

Combine sugar, hot water and corn syrup in a heavy one- or two-quart saucepan. Place on high heat and stir with a wooden spoon until all sugar crystals are dissolved. Wash down sides of pan with a pastry brush dipped in hot water. Clip on thermometer. Continue cooking, without stirring, until thermometer registers 300°F, then remove from heat.

Let stand until bubbles disappear. Add flavoring and food color and stir to blend. Pour into prepared molds. Let harden at room temperature about ten minutes. Turn molds over and press lightly with thumbs to pop out shapes onto paper towel. These will keep at room temperature for up to six weeks. Keep well-covered with plastic wrap to avoid stickiness. Yield: about 25 small shapes

Apricot glaze

Heat one cup of apricot preserves to boiling, strain, then brush on cake while still hot. It will dry to a hard finish in 15 minutes or less. This is good to crumb-coat cakes before icing, adding a trace of tangy flavor. Use it also for Australian or English method cakes.

Wilton basic marzipan

Use this for the first covering of Australian or English method cakes. Makes beautiful modeled flowers, too.

16 ounces almond paste

4 eggs whites, unbeaten

1 teaspoon vanilla or rum flavoring

6½ cups sifted confectioners' sugar (approximate)

Crumble almond paste in a large mixing bowl. Add egg whites and flavoring and knead until thoroughly mixed. Now add the sugar, a cup at a time, and knead very thoroughly after each addition until no lumps remain. Add enough sugar to the mixture so that marzipan has the texture of heavy pie dough. The entire process will take about 20 minutes.

NOTE: you may mix almond paste, egg whites, flavoring and 2 or 3 cups of the sugar in an electric mixer at low speed. Then add remaining sugar and knead by hand. This will shorten the procedure.

Wrap closely in plastic wrap, then put in a tightly closed container and store for months in the refrigerator. When ready to use, bring to room temperature and knead again. If marzipan is too stiff, knead in a drop or two or warmed corn syrup until original consistency is restored. Yield: enough to cover a 10″ round cake.

TO ROLL OUT marzipan, dust work surface and rolling pin with a sifting of confectioners' sugar. Roll out just like cookie or pie dough.

Best-ever fruitcake

Ideal for Australian and English method cakes. Rich and delicious!

3 cups all-purpose flour

2 teaspoons baking soda

1 teaspoon baking powder

½ teaspoon cloves

½ teaspoon nutmeg

½ teaspoon cinnamon

½ teaspoon salt

1 pound candied cherries

½ pound mixed candied fruit

8 ounces candied pineapple

¾ cup dates

1 cup raisins

1½ cups chopped pecans (6-ounce package)

1½ cups chopped walnuts (6-ounce package)

½ cup butter

1 cup sugar

2 eggs (Grade A large)

½ cup white grape juice

1½ cups applesauce (16-ounce can)

Preheat oven to 275°F. Sift and mix first seven ingredients. Cut up fruit and mix with nuts. Stir one cup of the sifted dry ingredients into fruit-nut mixture.

Cream butter and sugar. Add eggs and beat well. Beating until blended after each addition, alternately add remaining dry ingredients and grape juice to the creamed mixture. Mix in fruit-nut mixture and applesauce. Turn into pan sprayed with non-stick pan release. Bake at 275°F. for two and a half hours. Run a knife around sides of pan and let cake cool ten minutes in pan. Remove cake and cool thoroughly. Yield: a cake baked in an 10½″ ring pan, or 10″ x 3″ springform pan.

Baking and preparing the tiers

WHAT RECIPE TO USE? Almost any mix or recipe is suitable—consult the bridal couple for their preferences. If you plan to cover the cake with rolled fondant, be sure to use a firm pound cake, applesauce or fruit cake.

HEIGHT OF THE BAKED TIERS is important. If tiers are not high enough, the finished cake will be out of proportion, and perhaps not allow you enough space for side trims. Always consult the directions for the cake design you have chosen for correct tier height. Most lower, two-layer tiers are 4″ high, each layer 2″ high. Two-layer top tiers are usually 3″ high—but there are many exceptions to these rules. Your own experience is the best guide for amounts of batter to use—but the chart at right will give you approximate amounts of cake mix for various sizes of pans.

LEVEL TIERS ARE ESSENTIAL for your masterpiece, so follow these tips to achieve them. After you've filled the pans with batter, lift them a few inches above the counter and drop. Now swirl batter from center to sides of pan. Finally,

dampen 2″ strips of terry cloth (cut from an old towel) and pin around outside of pans. Some decorators have found that setting the oven heat 25°F below that called for in the recipe, then baking for a longer period is helpful.

WHEN LAYERS ARE BAKED, cool in pan ten minutes, run knife around edges and turn out of pan on towel-covered rack. Immediately, put a second rack on top of layer, and turn over to cool completely. Layer will be right side up, with no rack marks.

ALWAYS CHILL OR FREEZE the baked layers on racks before icing. Wrap them closely in wax paper or plastic wrap. This makes them much easier to handle and allows you to bake them some days ahead of decorating time. If the layers are still not level, it is easy to trim them now with a long serrated knife. Allow frozen layers to thaw, still wrapped, an hour or less before icing.

ATTACH CARDBOARD CAKE CIRCLE, the same size, under bottom layer of every tier before icing. This circle makes it easier to move the

tier, easier to separate stacked tiers for serving, and prevents knife scratches on tray or separator plate when the tier is being cut. Here's how to do it.

Lay wax paper on top of chilled layer, then place a cardboard cake circle, same size or larger, on the wax paper, and turn over. Remove rack. Put a few dabs of royal icing on the bottom of the layer (now on top). Attach cardboard cake circle, same size as layer. Turn over again and set on turntable to ice. Remove circle and wax paper. This method also applies to iced tiers. Just let the icing crust before moving.

APPROXIMATE AMOUNTS OF CAKE MIX FOR LAYERS*	
Pan size	Amt. of batter
6″ x 2″	1 cup plus 2 tablespoons
8″ x 2″	2¼ cups
10″ x 2″	1 package
12″ x 2″	1 package plus 2 cups
14″ x 2″	2 packages
16″ x 2″	3 packages
12″ x 18″ x 2″	3 packages

* Approximate amount of batter in one package is 4 cups plus 2 tablespoons

Icing the tiers

Always place the tier on a turntable to ice. It will make your work much quicker and easier. For most cakes, use buttercream. It is delicious, may be flavored in many ways and is very easy to smooth onto the tiers.

PIPE A THICK RING OF ICING around top edge of layer, then spread filling or icing inside ring. Place cake circle on top of chilled top layer, leaving a little of the top uncovered. Turn over as described for bottom layer above. Rest uncovered portion of upside down top layer on edge of bottom layer and slowly slide cake circle out until top layer rests entirely on bottom layer. Brush crumbs from tier, then brush with apricot glaze to seal in any other crumbs. Or spread with a thin layer of icing. Dry until a crust forms, about 10 minutes.

Classic way of icing a tier

COVER TIER, using long, even strokes. Spread plenty of icing on side with a long spatula, building up edges slightly higher than cake. Work from the bottom up. Mound icing in center of top and spread to blend with edges.

SMOOTH TOP using a long metal ruler or piece of stiff cardboard. Pull straight across tier, bringing excess icing toward you. To smooth sides, hold spatula against cake side and slowly spin turntable. When icing sets, remove tier to tray, cake board or separator plate.

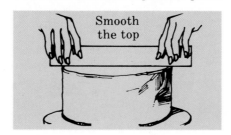
Smooth the top

New quick Wilton method

COVER THE TOP of the tier first, in the classic way. To cover the side of the tier, use a 16″ decorating bag and "cake icer" tube 789. Fill the bag, then pipe a strip of icing around lower part of tier. Pipe a second strip to cover upper part of tier, overlapping as necessary. Smooth the top, as shown below. Smooth the side by holding a spatula against tier side as you spin turntable. You'll be surprised at how quickly the tier is smoothly iced.

Smooth the side

The dowel method of tier cake assembly

The secret behind most towering wedding cakes is a strong framework of wooden dowels. This framework allows you to carry the cake safely to the reception site, prevents the weight of the upper tiers from crushing those below, and keeps the tiers from shifting. So use dowels, avoid disaster!

Here we show you how to construct a three-tier cake, the base and middle tiers stacked. See the cake on page 59. The method will be the same regardless of the number of tiers, or whether they are stacked or separated by pillars. Every tier should contain dowel supports, except the top tier.

PREPARE CAKE BOARD. Use three or more thicknesses of corrugated cardboard. Or, for a large heavy cake, use masonite or plywood. Cut the cake board 2″ larger all around than the base tier. Cover smoothly with foil. Cut the foil 4″ larger than the board, fold around the edge and tape underneath.*

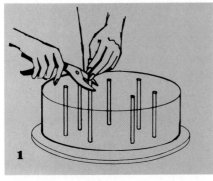

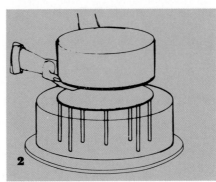

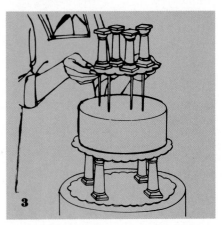

SECURE ICED BASE TIER to the cake board with dabs of royal icing. Using a cardboard cake circle one size smaller than the next tier, center it on the base tier and press it gently into icing, then remove, to mark an outline. If the second tier is 10″ or less, position seven ¼″ dowel rods within the outline. Use this as a rule: *the larger and more numerous the upper tiers, the more dowels needed.* Really big cakes need ½″ dowels in base tier. Push the dowels down into the tier to touch the base, then lift up and clip off the exposed portions with wire cutters or pruning shears. (Use a coping saw for ½″ dowels.) Push the dowels back into the tier until level with the top.

CENTER A CLEAR PLASTIC-WRAPPED CARDBOARD CAKE CIRCLE, same size as middle tier, on base tier. Place middle tier on base tier, attaching with royal icing. (The plastic will not stick to icing on base tier when middle tier is removed for slicing.) Center a cardboard cake circle one size smaller on top of the middle tier. Press lightly into the icing, then remove to mark an outline. If the next tier or plate is 8″ or less, position five dowel rods within the outline. For larger tiers, use more dowels. Push down to cardboard beneath tier, then lift, clip exposed portions and push back into tier so they are level with the surface. To prevent tiers from slipping sideways, sharpen a long ¼″ dowel rod, push through center of both tiers and clip off level with top of middle tier.

POSITION SEPARATOR PLATE, with pillars and pegs in place, by pushing the pegs into the tier until the plate rests on top. (Pegs are supplied with plates.) When decorating, pipe a border around edge of plate for a neat, trim effect.

FINALLY, PLACE TOP TIER ON ITS SEPARATOR PLATE, attaching with royal icing. Remove cardboard cake circle from under tier first, so the ridges on plate will hold tier securely. Position plate on the pillars. Now you are ready to start decorating. First measure and mark the tiers for position of trims. Then, either decorate the assembled cake, or take tiers apart to decorate tiers individually.

Add a ruffle to your cake board by pushing it under the base tier with a small spatula.

Constructing with clear dividers or the tall tier stand

Here are two other ways of assembling tiers that are very quick and easy. No dowels are needed to support weight.

Assembling with clear dividers

These clear legs and their accompanying plates give a very airy look to your cake. A good example is on page 114.

ATTACH ICED TIERS to plates with strokes of royal icing. The plate is usually 2″ larger than the tier. Attach base tier to cake board.

FIT THE CLEAR LEGS into the separator plates of the two upper tiers. Hold middle tier above base tier. Make sure it is centered, then, holding tier by edge of plate, push down until legs touch the cake board beneath base tier.

Hold top tier above middle tier, center, and push into middle tier. Be sure legs line up. Measure and mark tiers.

DECORATE THE ASSEMBLED CAKE, starting with base tier. Or you may remove plates from legs of two top tiers and decorate each tier individually.

Assembling with tall tier stand

Strong center columns elevate the tiers and provide good support. See the cake on page 45. Use tiers 2″ smaller in diameter than plates.

CUT A HOLE in the center of each corrugated cardboard cake circle needed for the tiers—16″, 12″ and 8″ for Butterfly, page 45. To position holes, fold paper circles the same size into quarters and snip points. Slip the circles over the lower end of one of the columns to make sure holes are large enough. Place paper circles on cardboard cake circles, mark positions of holes and cut out with a sharp knife. Save the paper circles. Place filled tiers on prepared cake circles and ice.

USING THE PAPER CIRCLES again, mark the position of hole in center of each lower tier. Cut holes in all lower tiers with a cake corer.

DECORATE AFTER CAKE IS ASSEMBLED. Place iced base tier on 18″ footed base plate. Insert column and screw to secure. Set 12″ tier on 14″ plate and secure column. Set 10″ plate on column and secure with nut. Set 8″ tier on 10″ plate. Measure and mark the tiers. Now decorate cake.

OR DECORATE TIER BY TIER. After tiers have been assembled and marked, take apart. Decorate base tier on its footed base plate. Set 12″ tier (on its plate) on a 12″ cake pan to steady as you decorate. Assemble tiers, then decorate top tier.

How the experts do it . . . quick and easy

READ ALL DIRECTIONS completely and thoroughly before starting to bake the tiers. The order in which you decorate is important for best results. And make sure all needed accessories are at hand.

ALWAYS ASSEMBLE the iced tiers completely before starting to decorate. This will give you a good view of the cake as it will appear on the reception table. Even more important, it will assure that the pillars are well lined up. As soon as the cake is assembled, *measure and mark the tiers*. Use a toothpick or tiny dot of icing to mark. Your borders, garlands and all other trim will be in the proper places. Also make a tiny mark to indicate the back of each tier. Decorate the assembled cake, or take the tiers apart to decorate individually.

MOST MEASURING IS EASY, and can be done by eye. If you can divide the measurements by four, the four pillars will be your guide. Just make a mark at the edge of the tier corresponding to each pillar, then divide the remaining space evenly.

If the cake has six pillars, measuring is even easier.

FOR COMPLEX MEASURING, the most practical tool we know consists of a large marked circle of sturdy clear plastic. A handy triangle comes with it. With this aid you can easily divide and mark a tier of any size.

START FROM THE BOTTOM and work up as you decorate the tiers. This is the correct procedure for all tier cakes, *except* when two or more tiers are stacked, without pillars. Then work from the upper stacked tier down to the one beneath it.

KEEP YOUR WORK AT EYE LEVEL as you decorate. This makes it easy to pipe evenly dropped strings and perfectly curved garlands and borders. If necessary, prop the cake upon a sturdy box or pile of books—or place it on a low table.

USE A COUPLER to speed your work. It lets you change tubes in a flash without changing your bag.

FOR PERFECT CURVED GARLANDS, always drop string guidelines first to define the curves. Use any small round tube.

STRINGWORK IS EASY if you pipe it in royal icing thinned with a little piping gel. White corn syrup works well, too. Use this on any cake, whatever its covering.

FOR CURVES ON TIER TOPS, mark lightly with a round cookie cutter of appropriate size.

FOR STRONGER LATTICE and lace pieces, thin meringue royal icing with a little egg white.

ATTACH TOP TIER to a foil cake board before putting it on a separator plate. Then it will be easy to present to the bride.

ADD PIPED FLOWERS LAST, after all other trim has been completed. Work from the top tier down. Use smaller flowers for upper tiers, larger ones for lower tiers. And don't forget to trim the ornament with flowers, too, When all flowers are in place, pipe leaves.

Assembling tier cakes with filigree stairways

Filigree stairways give a dramatic, important look to any tier cake—and they are truly effortless to use.

When to use stairways

MOST STAIRWAY SPECTACULAR cakes are designed to join two or more cakes for a single lacy vision on the reception table. You'll see many of them in this book. Stairways are an ideal way to gain more servings from easy-to-bake smaller cakes—and make them much prettier and more imposing, too.

EVEN A SINGLE CAKE may be ornamented with a stairway. See the lovely one on page 72.

MANY TYPES OF CAKES look more important with a stairway. It's an outstanding accessory for a graduation cake, a shower cake or a cake celebrating a promotion or achievement. Stairways are perfect for anniversary cakes.

THE BRIDGE IS USEFUL in many ways, even without the stairways. Use it as a dainty base for a bridal or anniversary couple, a cupid figure, even a bouquet. Set it on top of the cake or within pillars.

KEEP THE HEIGHT OF YOUR TIERS in mind when you plan to add a stairway. The easiest way to do this is to construct the cake the same as one of those pictured in this book. Of course you may vary the trim as you wish.

How to attach the stairway

You'll find this very easy. It's handy to have a friend hold the stairway as you shift position of the cakes.

WHEN STAIRWAY AND BRIDGE ARE JOINED. Just slide the tops of the stairways into the slots below the surface of the bridge. Set main cake and satellite cakes in approximate position. Ask your helper to hold the assembled stairway and bridge above the cakes. Shift the satellite cake (or cakes) as necessary. Gently press the bridge until its base touches the top tier of the main cake. Allow the bottom of the stairway to rest on the satellite cake.

WHEN USING STAIRWAY ONLY. Arrange main cake and satellite cake (or cakes) in approximate positions. Hold stairway above cakes and shift the cakes as necessary. Gently press top of stairway into top of main cake until stairway is level with top surface. Allow bottom of stairway to rest on satellite cake.

How to design your own stairway spectacular

It's simple to work the stairway into your own original cake design. Study the diagrams at right for ideas. Keep only two measurements in mind:

1. *Allow for an 8" difference* in height from top to bottom of stairway *if you do not join* the stairway to the bridge.

2. *Allow for a 7" difference* in height from top to bottom of stairway *if you join* the stairway to the bridge.

Study these diagrams to plan correct heights of tiers when using stairways. Include height of pillars and cake stands.

Cakes with stairways not attached to bridge

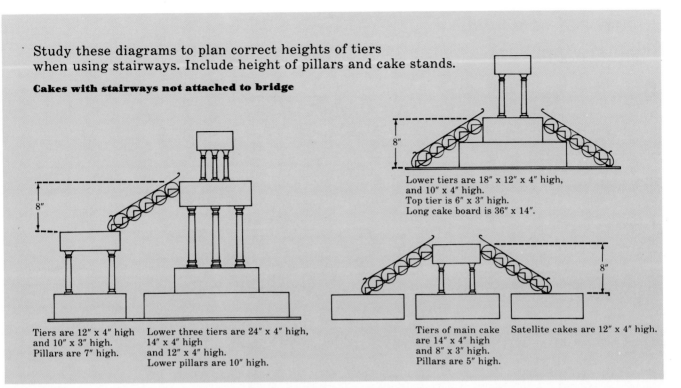

Tiers are 12″ x 4″ high and 10″ x 3″ high.
Pillars are 7″ high.

Lower three tiers are 24″ x 4″ high, 14″ x 4″ high and 12″ x 4″ high.
Lower pillars are 10″ high.

Lower tiers are 18″ x 12″ x 4″ high, and 10″ x 4″ high.
Top tier is 6″ x 3″ high.
Long cake board is 36″ x 14″.

Tiers of main cake are 14″ x 4″ high and 8″ x 3″ high.
Pillars are 5″ high.

Satellite cakes are 12″ x 4″ high.

Cakes with stairways attached to bridge

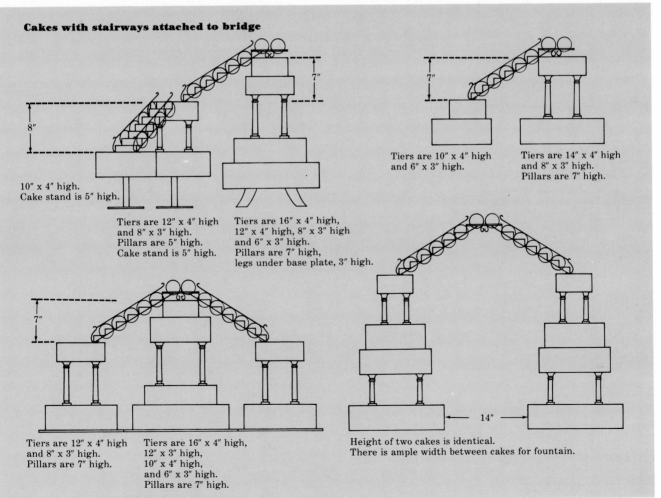

10″ x 4″ high.
Cake stand is 5″ high.

Tiers are 12″ x 4″ high and 8″ x 3″ high.
Pillars are 5″ high.
Cake stand is 5″ high.

Tiers are 16″ x 4″ high, 12″ x 4″ high, 8″ x 3″ high and 6″ x 3″ high.
Pillars are 7″ high, legs under base plate, 3″ high.

Tiers are 10″ x 4″ high and 6″ x 3″ high.

Tiers are 14″ x 4″ high and 8″ x 3″ high.
Pillars are 7″ high.

Tiers are 12″ x 4″ high and 8″ x 3″ high.
Pillars are 7″ high.

Tiers are 16″ x 4″ high, 12″ x 3″ high, 10″ x 4″ high, and 6″ x 3″ high.
Pillars are 7″ high.

Height of two cakes is identical.
There is ample width between cakes for fountain.

Amount of servings provided by tiers

Before you begin to plan your cake, find out the number of servings required. Then leaf through this book to decide on a design that provides approximately that number. Or create your own design, using this chart as reference.

Remember—the top tier of a wedding cake is usually frozen for the first anniversary. Therefore, do not include it in your estimate of servings.

Wedding and groom's cakes
Servings are 1″ wide by 2″ deep, two layers high.

SHAPE	SIZE	SERVINGS
ROUND	6″	16
	8″	30
	10″	48
	12″	68
	14″	92
	16″	118
	18″	148
SQUARE	6″	18
	8″	32
	10″	50
	12″	72
	14″	98
	16″	128
	18″	162
HEXAGON	6″	6
	9″	22
	12″	50
	15″	66
PETAL	6″	8
	9″	20
	12″	44
	15″	62
HEART	6″	12
	9″	28
	12″	48
	15″	90
RECTANGLE	9″x13″	54
	11″x15″	77
	12″x18″	108
OVAL	7″x9″	24

Shower and party cakes
Servings are ample dessert-sized portions, each two-layer

SHAPE	SIZE	SERVINGS
ROUND	6″	6
	8″	10
	10″	14
	12″	22
	14″	36
SQUARE	6″	8
	8″	12
	10″	20
	12″	36
	14″	42
RECTANGLE	9″x13″	24
	11″x15″	35
	12″x18″	54
HEART	6″	6
	9″	12
	12″	24
	15″	35
HEXAGON	6″	6
	9″	12
	12″	20
	15″	48
PETAL	6″	6
	9″	8
	12″	26
	15″	48
OVAL	7″x9″	12

How to cut a wedding or groom's cake

Two-layer servings, 1″ wide, 2″ deep.

START AT THE TOP. Remove the top tier and box for the bride. Remove the next tier down, taking off the pillars and separator plate on top of tier. Slice and serve. Continue working your way down the tiers. Base tier is cut last.

DIVIDE 7″ x 9″ OVAL TIERS vertically. Slice 1″ pieces within rows.

CUT HEXAGON TIERS like round tiers.

CUT PETAL TIERS like round tiers

DIVIDE HEART TIERS vertically. Slice 1″ pieces within rows.

CUT RECTANGULAR TIERS like square tiers.

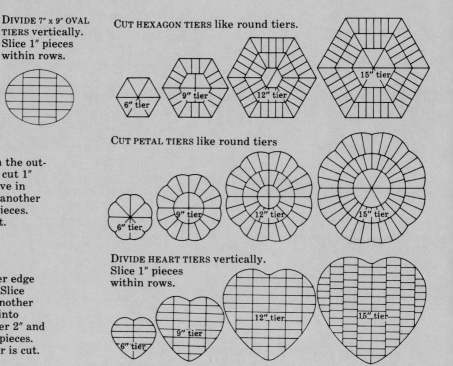

TOP VIEW OF 3-TIERED ROUND CAKE

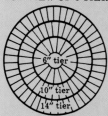

Move in two inches from the outer edge, cut a circle and cut 1″ wide slices within it. Move in another two inches, cut another circle, and slice into 1″ pieces. Continue until tier is cut.

TOP VIEW OF 3-TIERED SQUARE CAKE

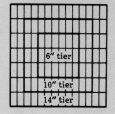

Move in 2″ from the outer edge and cut straight across. Slice into 1″ pieces. Move in another 2″ and slice this section into 1″ pieces. Move in another 2″ and slice this section into 1″ pieces. Continue until entire tier is cut.

Transport your cake this way in safety

Allow the icing to crust on the cake for at least half an hour after you have finished decorating.

1. Remove any tiers above pillars and remove pillars. These will be replaced on the reception table.

2. In large pieces of soft foam rubber, 3″ or 4″ thick, carve ½″ depressions, the exact size of your cake board and separator plates.

3. Set the foam rubber in the back of a station wagon. If you use a car for delivery, have a piece of plywood cut to fit the back seat. Level it securely with wood props.

4. Carefully set the tiers in the carved depressions of the foam rubber. Cover them with lightweight plastic bags (like those used by dry cleaners). Carry a stacked cake, without pillars, the same way, as a unit.

5. Drive with complete confidence to the reception site—even hundreds of miles away. Save the foam rubber pieces for delivery of future cakes.

Wilton ways with piped flowers

Piped flowers are the glorious trim on so many wedding cakes that it's wise to learn a few methods that show them off at their dainty best.

Flowers and leaves on stems

By mounting flowers on wire stems, then adding leaves on stems, you can arrange them even more easily than real flowers. Make a bouquet in a little bowl to set within pillars, form a graceful spray, or fashion a nosegay for the cake top.

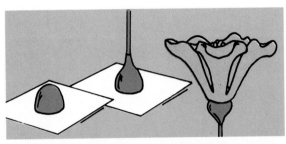

ADD STEMS TO FLOWERS. *Use only royal icing flowers.* On a square of wax paper, pipe a ball of green royal icing. Use the tube that corresponds to the weight of the flower—tube 4 for a daisy, tube 6 for a rose piped with tube 104. Insert a length of florists' wire into the ball, then brush the icing up on the wire to form a calyx. Use a damp brush. Stick the other end of the wire into a block of styrofoam to dry calyx.

Remove wax paper square and pipe a dot of royal icing on calyx. Gently press dried flower to icing and push stem into styrofoam to dry stemmed flower.

PIPE LEAVES ON STEMS. Use royal icing and any leaf tube. Work on a length of wax paper. Pipe a dab of icing on the paper, then lay a length of fine florists' wire on it. Pipe the leaf directly over the wire, so the center vein of the leaf corresponds to the wire. Let leaves dry thoroughly.

USE AN ASSEMBLY-LINE technique to stem many flowers and leaves in a short time. Arrange flowers and leaves by twisting stems together, then binding with floral tape. To make a cluster of leaves, put several together, then bind with floral tape.

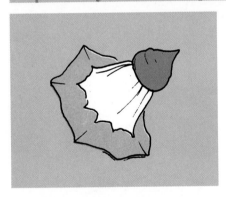

Attach flowers to tier sides

It's easy to secure a flower firmly to the side of a tier. *Use only royal icing flowers.* When flower has dried, turn over and pipe a spike on the back with royal icing. Use tube 4, 6 or 7—depending on weight of the flower. Let spike dry. To attach to side of tier, pipe a little icing around the spike, then push into the side of the tier.

SMALL LIGHTWEIGHT FLOWERS, like drop flowers, daisies or sweet peas, may simply be secured to the tier side with dots of icing.

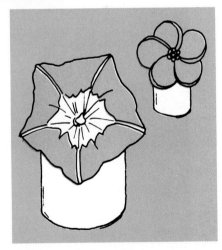

Lift up your flowers

To lift a flower above the surface of a tier to show it off, use the simple marshmallow. Ice a marshmallow to the tier, then secure the flower to it with a mound of icing. Conceal the marshmallow with more flowers and leaves. Use either full-size or miniature marshmallows and flowers made from royal, boiled or buttercream icing.

Appendix

Here are all the full-size patterns you need to create any cake in this book. To use the patterns, first trace them accurately on parchment paper.

FOR LACE PIECES, parts of lattice ornaments, lace wings or other flat items, tape the pattern to a stiff surface such as a piece of glass or plexiglass, then tape wax paper smoothly over the pattern. Pipe the design. To remove the piped design, cut the wax paper from the surface with an artist's knife. Cover the glass with a piece of foam toweling, then a piece of stiff cardboard. (Cake boards are handy for this.) Turn this "sandwich" over and piped pieces will be upside down. Carefully peel off the wax paper.

For very light pieces, such as tiny lace, simply cut the wax paper on two adjacent sides, and slide a piece of writing paper under the wax paper. Piped designs will loosen.

FOR DESIGNS PIPED DIRECTLY ON CAKE, first let the icing crust. Cut out the traced design. Hold or pin it to the cake surface and trace around it with a pin or toothpick. For complicated designs, it is easier not to cut the tracing out. Just lay it on the cake and prick through the design at close intervals with a pin.

FOR ROLLED FONDANT or gum paste designs, transfer the pattern accurately to light cardboard and cut out. Lay the pattern on the rolled fondant or gum paste and cut around it.

YOU'LL FIND MANY USES for your patterns for future cakes. Save them, carefully labeled, in an envelope.

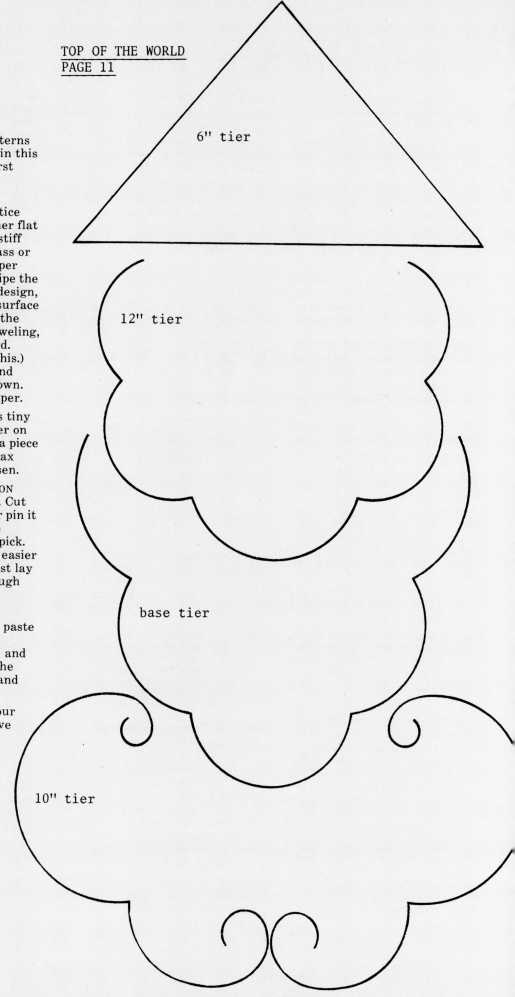

6" tier

12" tier

base tier

10" tier

172

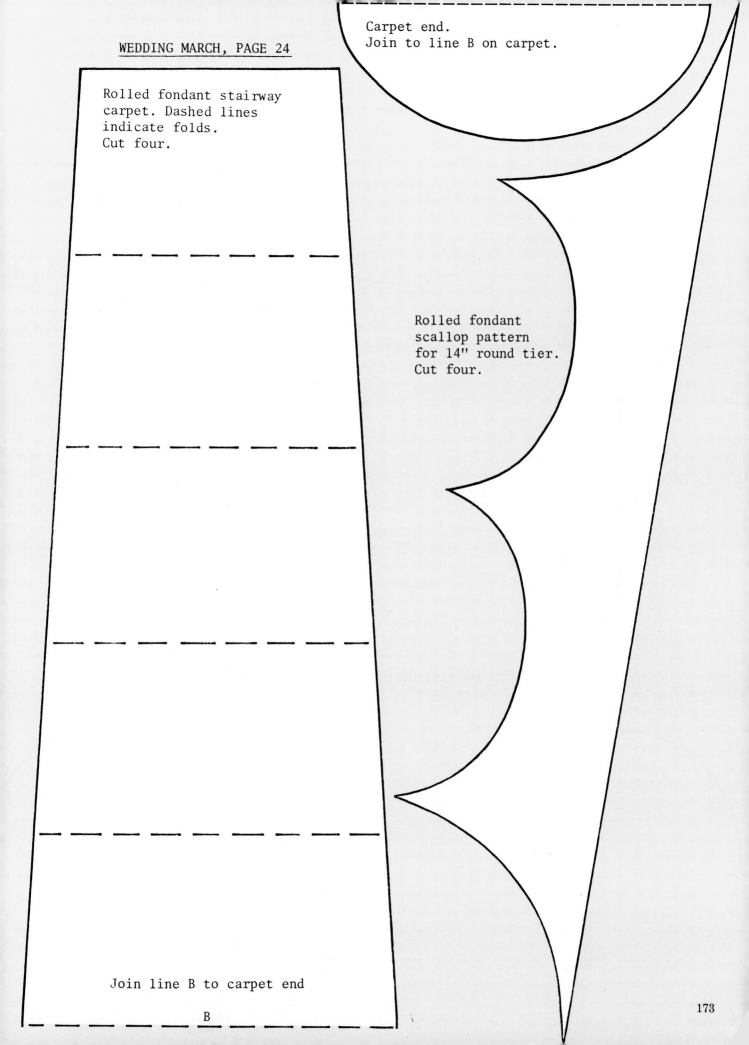

Rolled fondant stairway
carpet. Dashed lines
indicate folds.
Cut four.

Carpet end.
Join to line B on carpet.

Rolled fondant
scallop pattern
for 14" round tier.
Cut four.

Join line B to carpet end

B

One-fourth of pattern for 14" tier, main cake.

One-half of pattern for 10" tier, main cake.

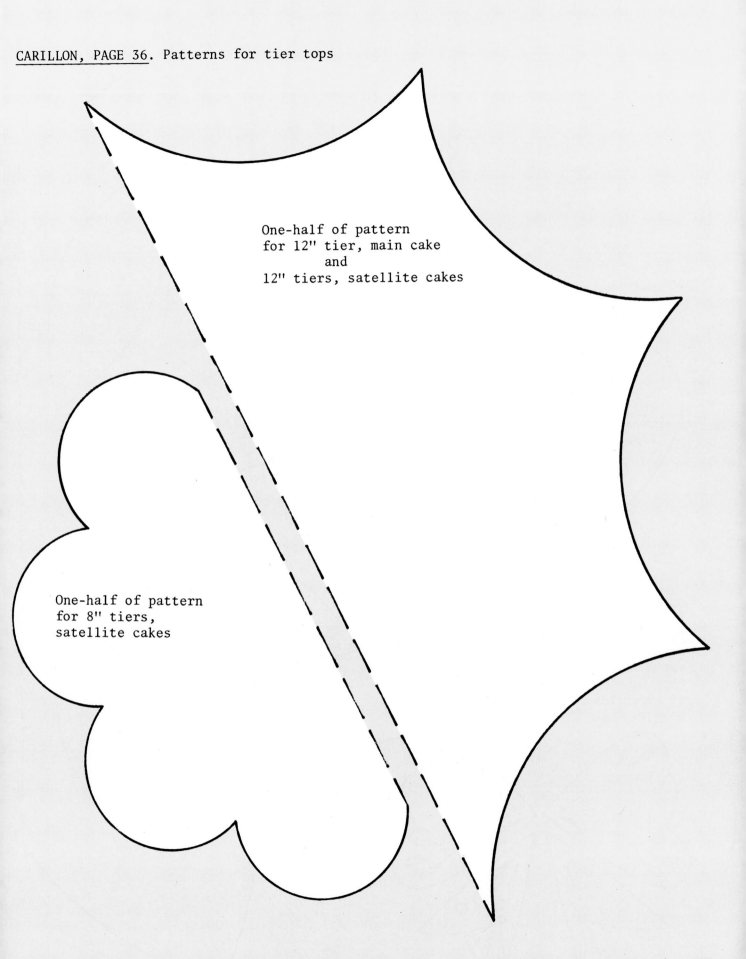

One-half of pattern
for 12" tier, main cake
and
12" tiers, satellite cakes

One-half of pattern
for 8" tiers,
satellite cakes

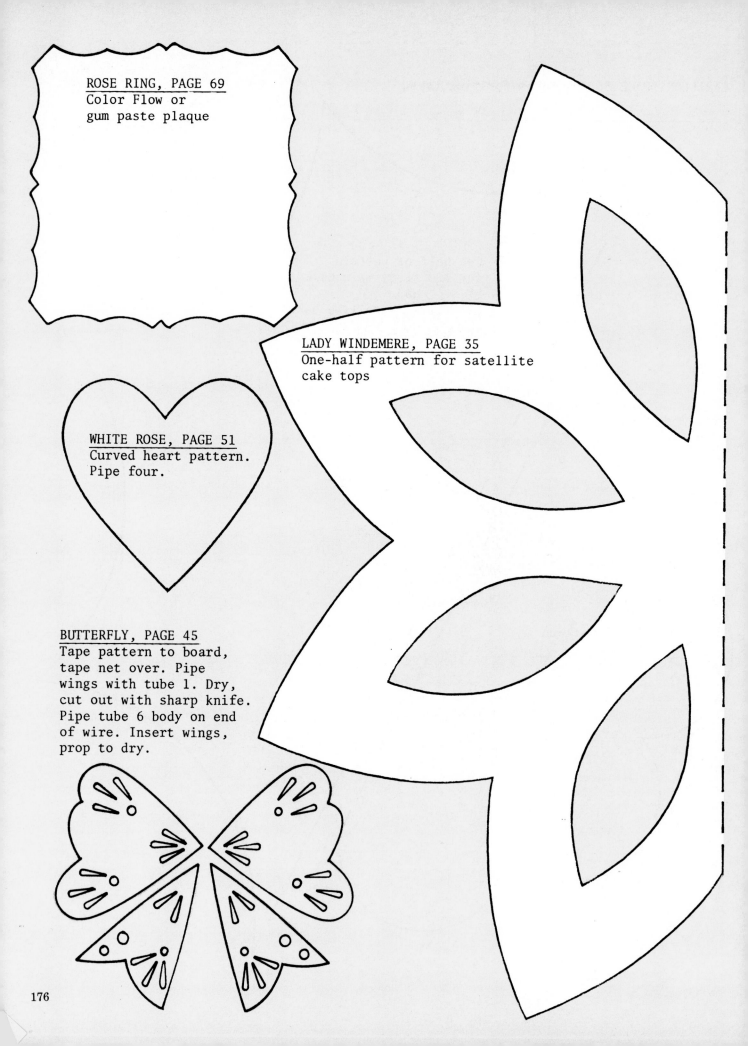

ROSE RING, PAGE 69
Color Flow or
gum paste plaque

LADY WINDEMERE, PAGE 35
One-half pattern for satellite
cake tops

WHITE ROSE, PAGE 51
Curved heart pattern.
Pipe four.

BUTTERFLY, PAGE 45
Tape pattern to board,
tape net over. Pipe
wings with tube 1. Dry,
cut out with sharp knife.
Pipe tube 6 body on end
of wire. Insert wings,
prop to dry.

One-half of upper base.
Cut 1/8" thick from gum paste

Ornament leaves. Pipe six

Ornament
wall section.
Pipe six

One-half of
ornament roof.

Cut from gum paste
1/16" thick

Wings for 12" tier.
Pipe twelve

Ornament wings.
Pipe six

Pattern for lower base and wall support
Lower base is ½" thick
Wall support is 1/8" thick

177

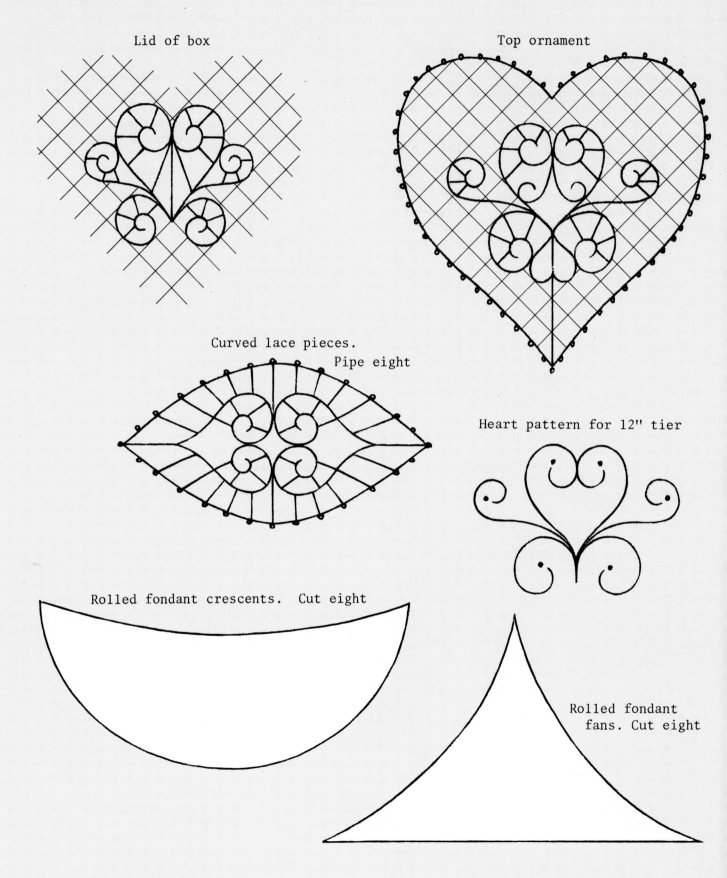

Lid of box

Top ornament

Curved lace pieces.
Pipe eight

Heart pattern for 12" tier

Rolled fondant crescents. Cut eight

Rolled fondant
fans. Cut eight

Heart pattern, lower tier

Scroll pattern, lower tier

Scroll pattern,
top tier

Lace pieces, lower tier

Lace pieces, top tier

Lattice side of
bird cage. Pipe six

Scrolls for roof of bird cage. Pipe twelve

Scrolls for base of bird cage. Pipe six

Scrolls for fence. Pipe six

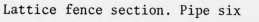

Lattice fence section. Pipe six

Lattice roof
of bird cage.
Pipe six

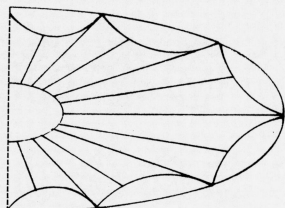

Two-piece oval side piece. Pipe six

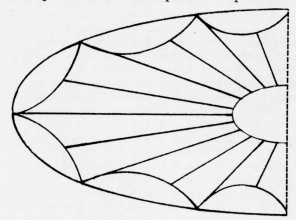

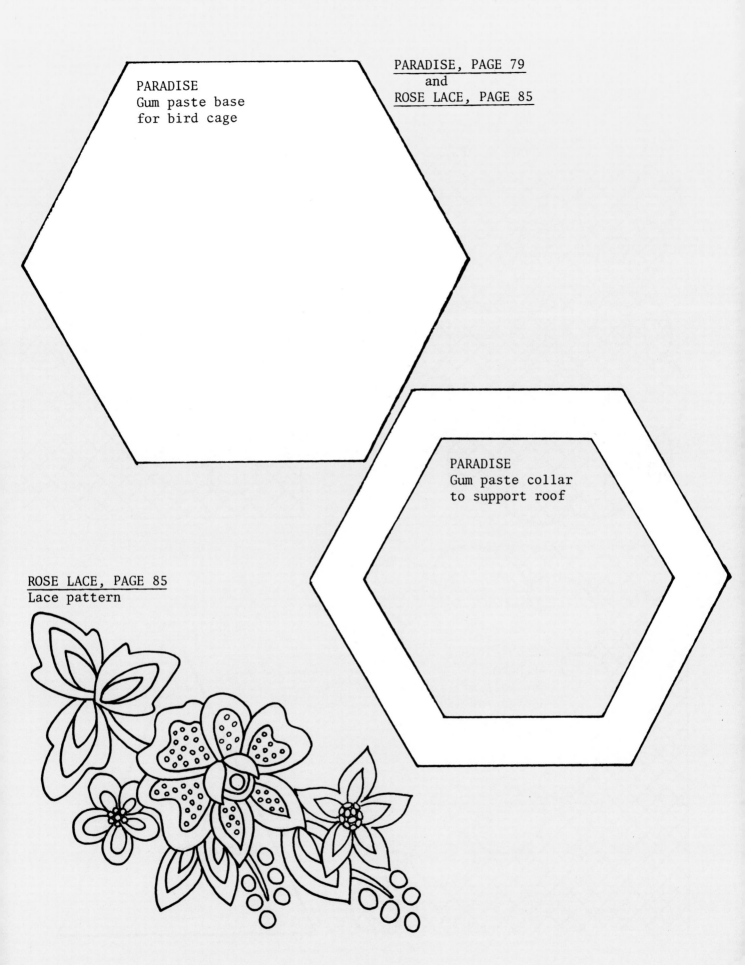

PARADISE
Gum paste base
for bird cage

PARADISE, PAGE 79
and
ROSE LACE, PAGE 85

PARADISE
Gum paste collar
to support roof

ROSE LACE, PAGE 85
Lace pattern

ALLEGRO
Lattice design
for 12" tier.
Pipe six

ALLEGRO
Lattice designs
for 9" tier.
Pipe six
of each

ALLEGRO
One-half of lattice
design for 15" tier.
Flop for second half.
Pipe six of each

SUNRISE, PAGE 89

Pattern for 6" tier

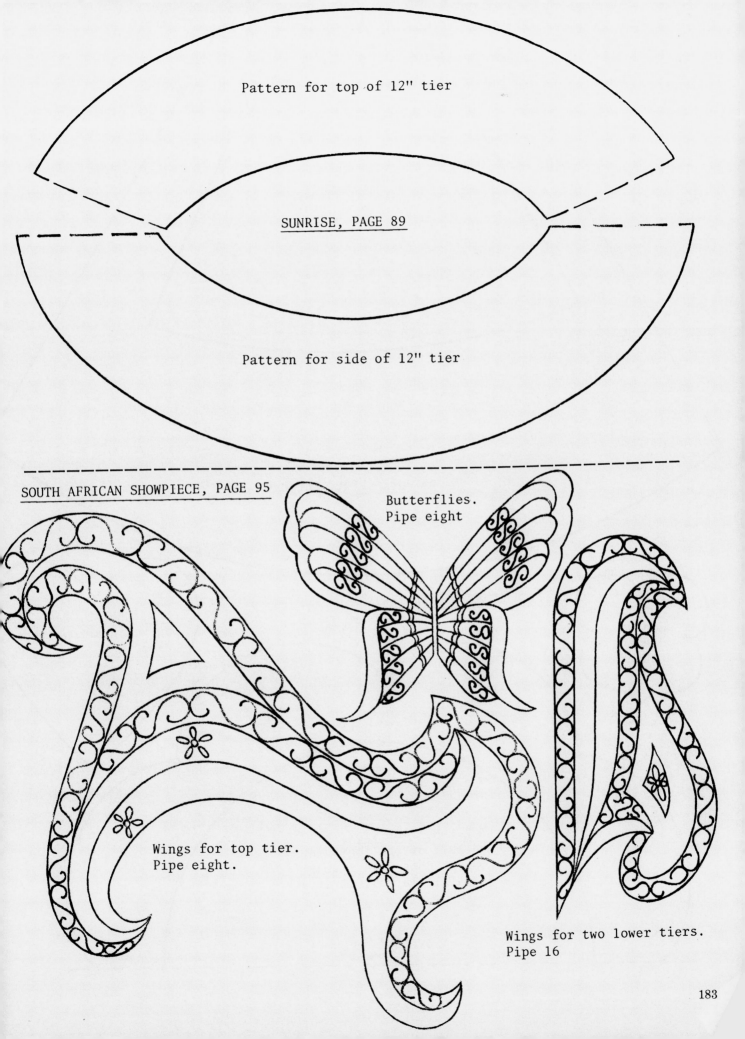

Pattern for top of 12" tier

SUNRISE, PAGE 89

Pattern for side of 12" tier

SOUTH AFRICAN SHOWPIECE, PAGE 95

Butterflies.
Pipe eight

Wings for top tier.
Pipe eight.

Wings for two lower tiers.
Pipe 16

183

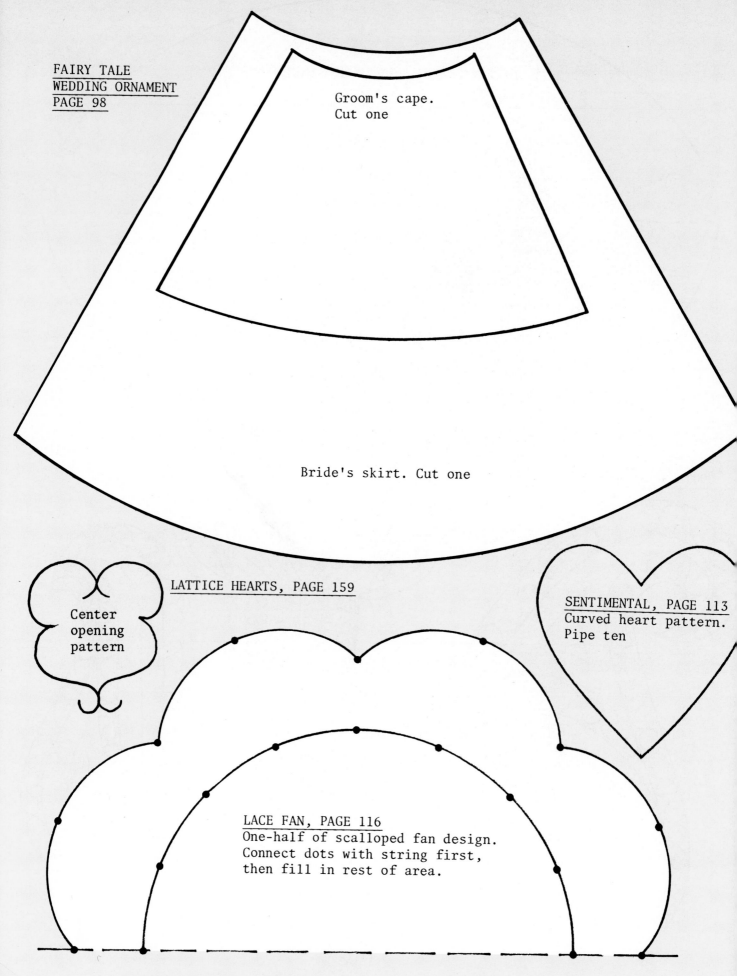

FAIRY TALE
WEDDING ORNAMENT
PAGE 98

Groom's cape.
Cut one

Bride's skirt. Cut one

LATTICE HEARTS, PAGE 159

Center
opening
pattern

SENTIMENTAL, PAGE 113
Curved heart pattern.
Pipe ten

LACE FAN, PAGE 116
One-half of scalloped fan design.
Connect dots with string first,
then fill in rest of area.

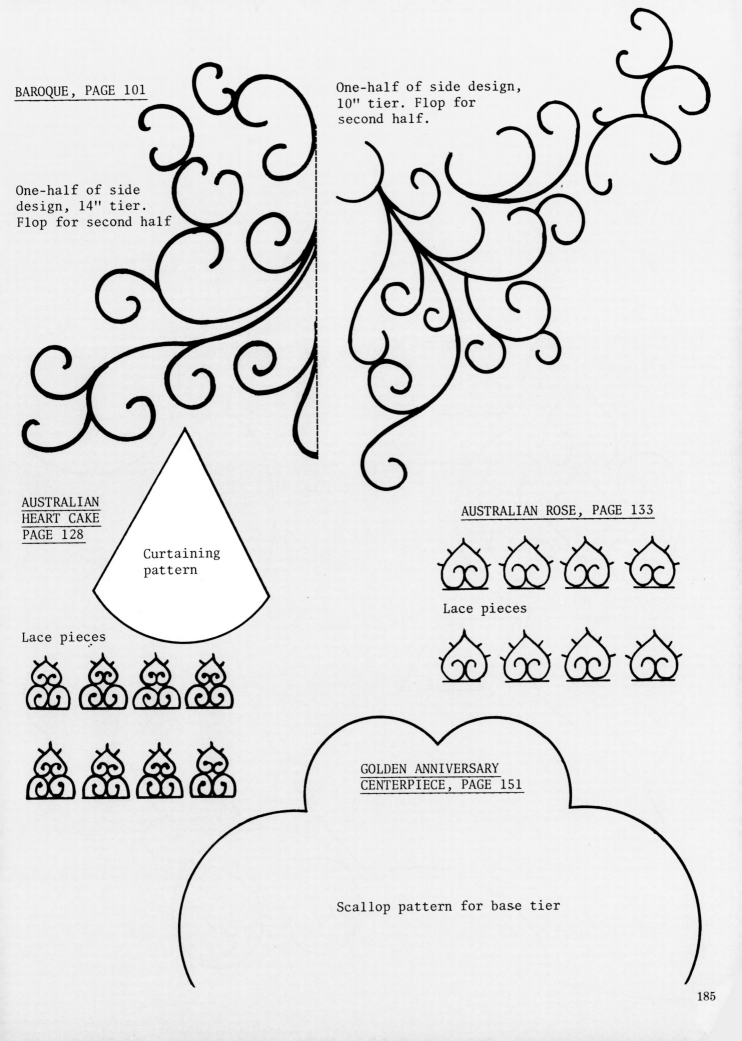

BAROQUE, PAGE 101

One-half of side design, 10" tier. Flop for second half.

One-half of side design, 14" tier. Flop for second half

AUSTRALIAN
HEART CAKE
PAGE 128

Curtaining pattern

Lace pieces

AUSTRALIAN ROSE, PAGE 133

Lace pieces

GOLDEN ANNIVERSARY
CENTERPIECE, PAGE 151

Scallop pattern for base tier

One-half of top pattern.
Flop for second half.

One-half of pattern
for plaque and
plaque supports

Curved side scroll

Curved base scrolls

EDWARDIAN ROSE, PAGE 120

Side design
for both tiers

One-fourth of design
for 9"x13"
tier top

40TH ANNIVERSARY CAKE, PAGE 139

JULY ANNIVERSARY
CAKE, PAGE 144

Plaque pattern

Gum paste plaque

One-half of scallop
pattern for 12" tier top

Ornament pattern.
Pipe six

Lace wings, pipe six

Upper tier pattern

Lace pieces

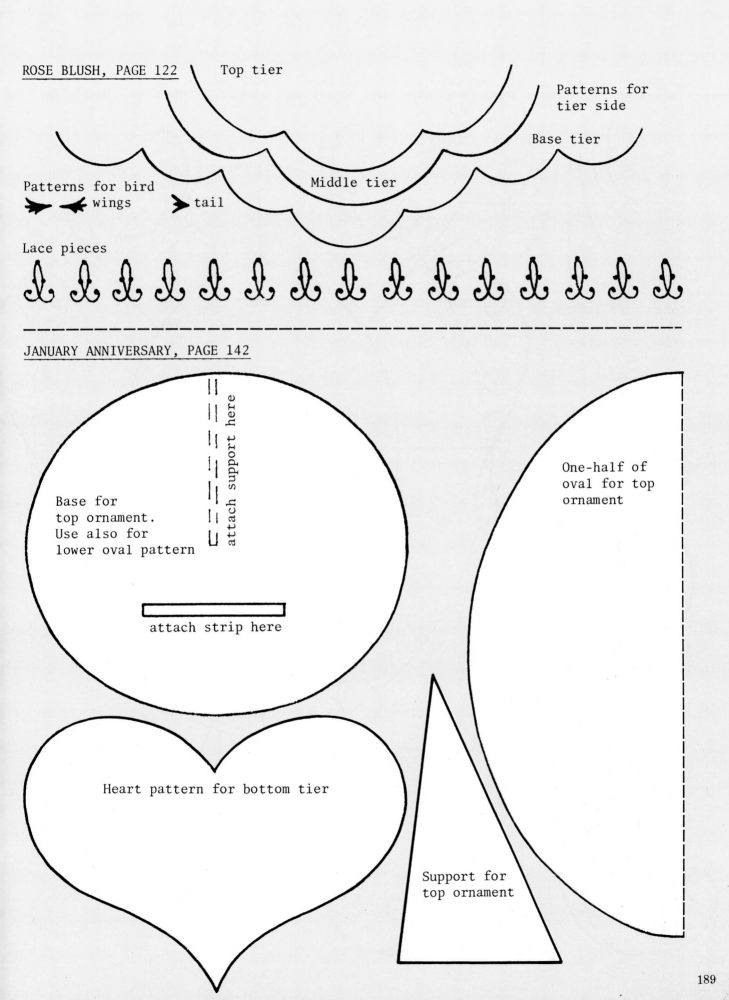

ROSE BLUSH, PAGE 122   Top tier

Patterns for
tier side

Base tier

Patterns for bird
wings   tail

Middle tier

Lace pieces

JANUARY ANNIVERSARY, PAGE 142

attach support here

Base for
top ornament.
Use also for
lower oval pattern

One-half of
oval for top
ornament

attach strip here

Heart pattern for bottom tier

Support for
top ornament

Side pattern
for top tier
(broken line indicates
base of top tier,
section of pattern
below that line
rests on top
of lower tier)

Cake-top frame

Use center oval
for plaque pattern

Numbers for
cake-top plaque

Side design
for lower tier

Jade heart.
Make one

Jade ovals.
Make five

20th ANNIVERSARY, PAGE 146

Gum paste oval.
Cut four

Gum paste heart.
Cut eight

Cut four

A SHOWER OF VIOLETS, PAGE 160

Large parasol

Small parasol

Cut in half for
half-parasol

TASSEL-TIED SHOWER CAKE, PAGE 154

Oval for base tier

Lattice fence. Pipe six

VIOLET NOSEGAY, PAGE 158

Lace pieces

CHOCOLATE ROSE, PAGE 152

One-half of
marzipan oval

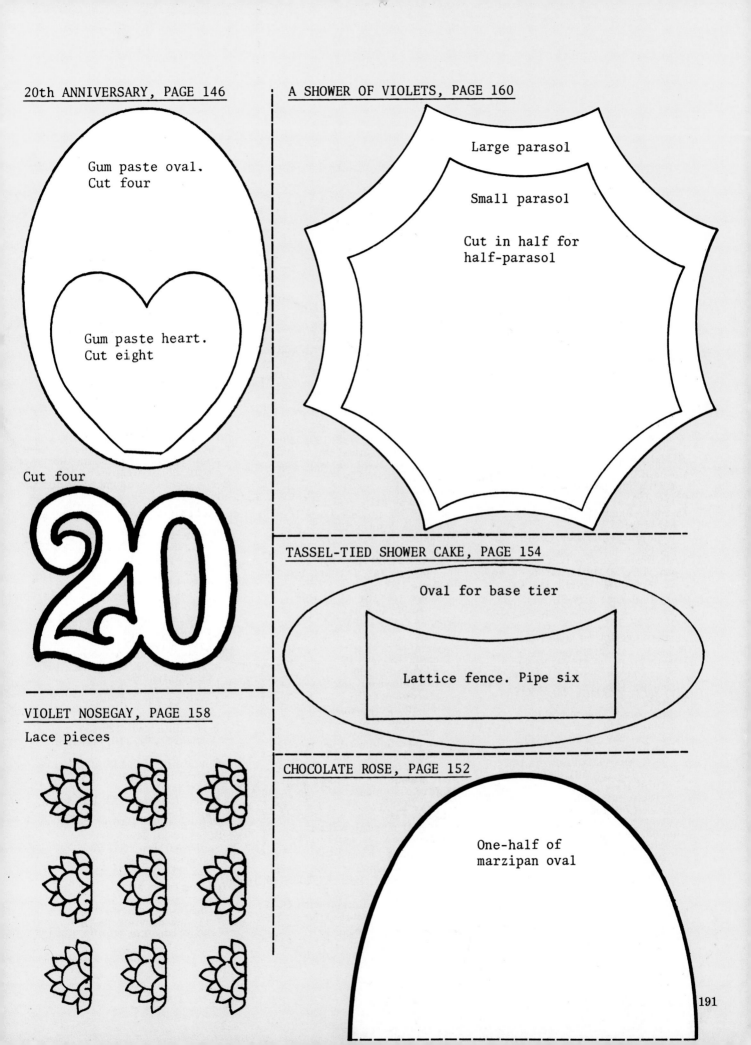

Index